Devotions for Hunters & Anglers
by
Tom C. Rakow, D.Min.

Devotions for Hunters & Anglers
Copyright © 2005 by Tom C. Rakow, D. Min.
Published by Rock Dove Publications
Silver Lake, MN 55381

All rights reserved. No part of this publication may be reproduced, stored in a retrieval system, or transmitted, in any form or by any means, electronic, mechanical, photocopying, recording, or otherwise, without the prior written permission of the publisher. Scripture quotations, unless otherwise noted, taken from the HOLY BIBLE, NEW INTERNATIONAL VERSION. Copyright © 1973, 1978, 1984 by International Bible Society.

ISBN 1-891147-50-1

Cover Photos: Meadowlark Lake, Wyoming; Dr. Tom C. Rakow and Gerry Caillouet host of *God's Great Outdoors Radio Broadcast* with fish in Ontario, Canada at Rushing Wind Retreat Center; Abigail Rakow with her first Minnesota black bear which field-dressed at 245#; whitetail doe in Kabatogema State Forest in Minnesota; Grace Rakow in South Dakota with the first fish she ever caught on a fly rod; Mercy Rakow acting as an excited young hunter with a tame deer at Paul Bunyan's Animal Land near Bemidji, Minnesota; Cookie the English pointer focused on doves; Faith Rakow and her dad with a big bass caught on a little pole; the late Bob Rakow with Andy and an evening's catch of raccoon in Wisconsin.

Dedicated to my dear friends and fellow laborers at Grace Bible Church in Silver Lake, Minnesota.

Acknowledgments

I am truly grateful for the many wonderful friends and family members with whom I have enjoyed hunts or fishing trips down through the decades. I contemplated listing some of these outdoor comrades, but I know that I would inadvertently leave out many. The years I spent hunting with my dad continue to conjure up heavenly thoughts. In fact, whenever I look up at a star-studded evening sky, I remember raccoon hunting with my dad. In recent years, hunting or fishing with my four daughters has truly been a wonderful experience. I only wish my dad could have gotten to go with them on a hunt or fishing trip. Although there are other hunting or fishing companions who have now left this world as well, the memories of the times we spent together will continue to live on. I have included a few of these events in this work, but many other episodes that transpired while hunting or fishing with other family members and friends will have to wait for another book.

Special thanks to my wonderful wife Beth for all the hard work she has invested in this book. I do realize you would have greatly preferred to have been working on one of your quilting projects. Thanks for going on that rabbit hunt back in 1988. I love you!

And, to my in-laws Dr. Phillip and Donna Wahlbeck: Thank your for your help in proofreading and other suggestions. As non-hunters and non-anglers I greatly appreciate your labor of love in reading things about which (apart from the biblical content) you are not personally interested.

Special thanks to Gerry Caillouet, Adam Doro, and Caara Holmstrom for their kind words about this book which are found on the back cover. Thank you for your encouragement.

I should also point out that, although there is much new material in this book, some of the entries were drawn or adapted from previous works I have written. These works include: *Devotions for Dog Lovers*, *Hunting & the Bible: A Scripture Safari*, and *Self-Inflicted Hunting Arguments: Biblical Responses to a Loaded Issue.* In addition, many other devotional entries initially appeared in various volumes of *Devotions for Deer Hunters* (a ministry tool of the Christian Deer Hunters Association®) and *Devotions for Anglers* (a ministry tool of the Christian Anglers Association). Therefore, those who have assisted with these previous works have also helped with this endeavor. Information about these books and organizations just mentioned can be found or accessed through the Rock Dove Publications website.

It should also become obvious to the reader that this author in no way claims to be an "expert". On the contrary, this book will probably make most anglers and hunters feel pretty good about their outdoor skills! It is my sincere hope that some of these stories will give you a good laugh or at least make you grin a little. But most of all, it is my prayer that you will have a greater understanding and desire to know Jesus Christ.

Lord Bless,
Tom C. Rakow, D.Min.

Table of Contents

Buck Fever 9
Live Bait 11
Grin and Bear It! 13
A Case of Pheasant Forensics................................16
Fishing with a Safety Pin 19
All Things Are Possible 22
Three Legs...24
A Secret Meant to Be Shared 26
Confessions of a Poacher......................................27
Where's that Pointer Pointing? 29
The Devil's Tackle Box...30
Things Are Not Always As They Appear....................31
The North American Hunter: An Endangered
    Species? (Part 1) 33
The North American Hunter: An Endangered
    Species? (Part 2) 34
How's Your Fishing Form?......................................35
Persistence Pays Off..36
Barnyard Buck...37
Just Float and Fish..39
Trapped...41
Little Windows of Opportunity 43
The Antlered Doe..44
Does God Care about Animals and Birds?..................47
One-Eyed...49
Lucky 51
Little Things Mean a Lot 54
Buck in the Shadows...56
False Pointing 58
The Coat..59
A Keeper? 62
Powder and Pull..64
Doing What God Designed 65
God Never Misses 66
The Snake..68

All Shaken Up 70
The Ancient Tradition of Hunting 72
Rabbit Hunt Romance 73
God in the Ordinary 76
Sign 78
The Bible and Modern Hunting Weapons 79
Who Owns the Land? 80
Old Fishermen Never 82
The Great Divide 84
Old Antlers Never Die . . .But They Will Burn! 86
Sincerity Isn't Enough 88
The Vision 89
Divine Dividend 91
The Unseen Battle 94
Faith: An Essential Ingredient 95
It Was a Dark and Stormy Night 96
Counting the Cost 98
The Prodigal Pooch 100
I Still Wish! 102
Was Jesus a Vegetarian? 103
Catfish Corner 105
My Claim to Fame 107
Elk Hunt 110
Off the Beaten Path 112
Once in a Lifetime Moose Hunt (Part 1) 114
Once in a Lifetime Moose Hunt (Part 2) 118
Meadowlark Lake 121

BUCK FEVER
Scripture Reading: Romans 8:1-11

I will long remember the opening day of my first deer season. A member of our hunting party kicked out a nice six-pointer to me which stopped broadside only yards away. You could not have asked for an easier shot.

However, for some reason I could not bring the rifle to my shoulder. Instead, I shot eight times from the hip hitting dirt and trees a few feet in front of me. I watched helplessly as the buck finally bounded out of sight.

This was my initial and (hopefully) most memorable experience with a severe case of the jitters commonly known as "buck fever." Perhaps there was a time when you had a touch of the fever yourself.

Those who are unfortunate enough to fall under the influence of "buck fever" have been known to do such strange things as: shout "bang! bang!," lever unfired rounds on the ground, and yell for a deer to stop without firing a single shot. I even remember reading of one hunter who downed his deer and then ran to put the tag on. He ended up with his deer, but two broken legs as well. In all the excitement he forgot he was in a tree stand more than fifteen feet off of the ground!

Nevertheless, as powerful as "buck fever" may seem, there is a force far stronger at work in our lives—an energy that frequently explodes and injures everyone with whom it comes in contact. This power that I'm referring to is not limited to a particular season of the year nor to a select group of people called "hunters." No, this destructive energy indwells and at times overrides every single member of the human race. Its name—the sinful nature.

But God has not left us helpless. He has provided a "helper." There is someone who will take up residence in our life and begin bringing the sinful nature under control. His name—the Holy Spirit.

If we have truly trusted Jesus Christ as our Savior, the Holy Spirit dwells inside of us and seeks to help us live lives that are pleasing to the Lord. As the apostle Paul told the believers in Rome, "You, however, are controlled not by the sinful nature but by the Spirit, if the Spirit of God lives in you. And if anyone does not have the Spirit of Christ, he does not belong to Christ" (Romans 8:9).

Prayer: *Father, help me to walk in the freedom that comes from Your Spirit. In Jesus' name. Amen.*

LIVE BAIT
Scripture Reading: Proverbs 7

A friend of mine loaned me a book that contains literally hundreds of pictures of old fishing lures. A couple of lures which incorporated the use of live minnows especially caught my attention. One was sold in the 1890's and consisted of a small glass tube with two hooks attached and on one end of the tube was a cork. In this way a live minnow was kept in the tube.

The other lure was produced in the 1930's and worked on the same principle. It was a small spring steel cage shaped like a minnow, and had treble hooks on each end of the cage. In both cases the use of a real "unharmed" minnow was used. Rather than put a hook through the minnow itself—an angler simply put a minnow into one of the lures.

It struck me that the devil often uses a similar strategy to hook humans. He will gain control of one life, and then use that control to capture yet another life.

For example, just as an angler will use a small live minnow to catch a bigger fish—so our adversary will often enlist someone from the opposite sex that he already controls in order to catch another soul or ruin a family. Of course this is a real danger for members of both sexes. However, it seems that men are especially susceptible to this type of seduction. In the Bible, great men like Samson, David, and Solomon were ensnared by their uncontrolled lusts for women. The book of Proverbs warns of how a young man can be led to ruin by an adulterous woman. We read,

> With persuasive words she led him astray; she seduced him with her smooth talk. All at once he followed her like an ox going to the slaughter, like a deer stepping into a noose till an arrow pierces his liver, like a bird darting into a snare, little knowing it

will cost him his life (Proverbs 7:21-23).

Nevertheless, taking heed to God's word can keep us from getting hooked. The Psalmist said, "How can a young man keep his way pure? By living according to your word" (119:9).

Prayer: *Heavenly Father, help me to always see and avoid temptations. I ask this in Jesus' name. Amen.*

GRIN AND BEAR IT
Scripture Reading: 1 Thessalonians 5:16-18

It was late afternoon on Thanksgiving Day and our little family (Beth, myself, and our young daughters) were in the parsonage alone enjoying a traditional turkey dinner. Beth noticed first—"You lost a tooth!" Sure enough a front tooth out of my lower plate was gone. Now I know that the Bible tells us to "give thanks in all circumstances, for this is God's will for you in Christ Jesus" (1 Thessalonians 5:18). And again the Scriptures say, "Do not be anxious about anything, but in everything, by prayer and petition, with thanksgiving, present your requests to God" (Philippians 4:6). Nevertheless, at that moment I was certainly not feeling very thankful, and I was worried.

I knew that losing an artificial tooth was not the end of the world. Call it vanity or just being self-conscious, however, as a pastor who would be standing up front preaching on Sunday I knew my missing tooth would certainly be visible. Furthermore, at that time we were about as financially strapped as a family could be paying school and medical bills, as well as driving a vehicle which was on its last leg. It would be quite a while before we could afford to have my plate fixed. What was I going to do?

For some unexplainable reason my thoughts started drifting to the freezer sitting in the garage. I especially started thinking about the black bear skull I had wrapped up in a black garbage bag.

At first I dismissed the idea. But, soon I found myself standing in the garage digging through the freezer. I removed the contents from the bag. Hmmm. The more I looked at the teeth in the skull, the more it seemed like a real possibility. I dashed to the tool box and pulled out a pair of pliers and got a sharp knife.

By that evening the tooth had been filed down to fit

in place and was firmly held with a glue mixture normally used by taxidermists. That first bear tooth lasted several months, then back to the freezer I went for another.

No one other than Beth and our girls knew about my unusual use of bear teeth until about six months later when I told my parents and siblings. Their initial responses to this strange revelation varied greatly. My dad thought it was hilarious, while mom expressed grave concern exclaiming, "You could get a disease or something!"

To which I responded, "Well, I have noticed that I want to sleep a lot, and I now have this strange desire to dig around in garbage cans." She didn't think it was very funny.

My sister Deb was primarily inquisitive. She peered into my mouth wondering exactly which tooth it was.

On the other hand, my brother Kelly said something which made me feel good. He asked if it was really true that I had a bear tooth. When I said, "Yes," he responded, "That's the kind of thing legends are made of!"

It was about a year-and-a-half before I finally got a new partial. But, I have to tell you that even now, years later, I am still grateful for that bear. In fact, God was thanked numerous times for that black bear. Not only was I grateful for the opportunity I had to harvest this creature (which was my first bear), but the Lord was also thanked at every meal where we served bear steaks, bear sausage, or bear burgers. Indeed, we found bear to be one of those foods "which God created to be received with thanksgiving" (1 Timothy 4:3b). But most of all I am thankful that this bear gave me the ability to grin without being too self-conscious. And, you never know, perhaps someday this same bear might even make me a legend!

Prayer: Lord, thank You for making teeth—all kinds of teeth! Amen.

A CASE OF PHEASANT FORENSICS
Scripture Reading: Hebrews 4:12-13

The ringneck rooster burst up out of the standing corn. I swung my twenty-gauge Beretta single shot to the shoulder—Boom! The bird folded—and fell to the ground.

My dad, older brother Mick, and I were hunting public land with a little black terrier named Smokey. Now Smokey worked well as a flush dog. You could always tell when Smokey was getting close to a pheasant—he would start yipping. And, when Smokey started yipping you better get ready because a pheasant was about ready to fly from its cover!

My brother and I both arrived at the downed pheasant at about the same time. But to my surprise Mick claimed "my" first pheasant as his! "What!" I said, "you didn't even shoot!" And, to my dismay, he said the same.

Now both of us were completely convinced that we had brought down the bird. However, dad pointed out that he heard us both shoot. In fact, our weapons went off so simultaneously that it was barely distinguishable that two different rounds from two different shotguns had been fired.

Eventually, Mick (who was six years older and far wiser) remarked that perhaps both of us hit him. He then suggested that when I cleaned the pheasant that an examination of the angle of entrance of the lead shot would make it obvious who made the kill. After all, he had shot from directly behind the bird—and I had fired from a quartering direction. In essence he was suggesting that I do some basic forensics on the pheasant.

I chose to take care of the pheasant the old-fashioned, tedious, and time consuming way we had always cleaned chickens. After dipping the rooster pheasant in scalding water, I started pulling feathers.

Nevertheless, the more wet feathers my thirteen year-old fingers plucked—the clearer certain undesirable facts came to light. First of all, my brother was the one who had shot the pheasant. Secondly, not a single BB from my pattern had even touched the bird. And, thirdly, I came to realize that my brother had slyly suckered me into cleaning a pheasant he had actually shot!

According to the Bible, unlike us, God sees and knows everything. This is the case whether it is a ringneck pheasant with all its feathers or a fully-clothed human standing in darkness. As the book of Hebrews states, "Nothing in all creation is hidden from God's sight. Everything is uncovered and laid bare before the eyes of him to whom we must give account" (Hebrews 4:13). And, as King David acknowledged in one of the Psalms, "If I say, 'Surely the darkness will hide me and the light become night around me,' even the darkness will not be dark to you; the night will shine like the day, for darkness is as light to you" (Psalm 139:11-12).

I don't know about you, but realizing that God sees and knows everything can be both a bothersome and a comforting thought. For example, it is bothersome and convicting to realize He sees our "secret" sins, but also comforting to know that He is aware of all our silent or unseen suffering.

Furthermore, in the future there is coming a time when everything we have ever done and why we did it will be exposed. Indeed, there is coming a day "when God will judge men's secrets through Jesus Christ" (Romans 2:16). Ultimately the curtain to each of our private lives and plans will be pulled back. All of our excuses will be plucked away. Yes, God will do His forensics. Nevertheless, if we know Christ as our Savior and are walking in fellowship with Him, we need not be terrified. However, knowing that someday everything is going to be exposed, we should be encouraged to live everyday in a way that is pleasing to Him.

Prayer: Lord, help me live in such a way that no matter where I may be, my life is pleasing to You. Amen.

FISHING WITH A SAFETY PIN
Scripture Reading: Hebrews 11:5-6

Doug was dirt poor, but suddenly he was admired by about every kid in our country school. He certainly did what very few of his classmates had ever accomplished during the noon recess. And, best of all, Doug did what he did without a rod, reel, or even a simple fish hook. Yes, Doug caught a sixteen-inch trout out of Bear Creek with a bent over safety pin and a few feet of fishing line—line he had borrowed from my older brother. You see, Doug's family was so poor he didn't own a Zebco® reel or any kind of fishing tackle. He didn't have much, but he used the little he had, and that's exactly what made Doug's feat so spectacular! After all, anyone can catch a rainbow or German brown on a regular pole. But, to catch a nice trout on a safety pin and little bit of line—wow! Why that's the stuff school legends are made of!

The fact is, we get inspired and encouraged by situations in which the person with little is able to accomplish much. We like seeing the incredible or the seemingly impossible achieved—especially by unlikely candidates. There is something inside each of us that makes us want to root for the underdog. We rejoice when the underachiever overcomes. We admire the person who perseveres despite prolonged or overwhelming obstacles. We look up to people like Joseph in the Old Testament who, despite years of suffering, ends up being promoted in a single day from prison to prime minister of Egypt (Genesis 41). We are amazed at Samson who, when the Spirit of the Lord comes upon him, is able to kill a thousand men with the fresh jawbone of a donkey (Judges 15). And, we adore seeing an insignificant orphan girl by the name of Esther become queen over an enormous empire (Esther 2).

Certainly, we all like to hear these kinds of David

and Goliath or rags-to-riches type stories. And, it is worth noting that the Bible is literally filled with those "who through faith conquered kingdoms, administered justice, and gained what was promised; who shut the mouths of lions, quenched the fury of the flames, and escaped the edge of the sword; whose weakness was turned to strength; and who became powerful in battle and routed foreign armies" (Hebrews 11:33-34).

However, such triumphs aren't just found in the pages of our Bible. We have reminders all around us of individuals who have attempted the impossible or accomplished the incredibly unlikely. Some have credited God with their victory, others their own stubborn tenacity.

Did you know that Dr. Seuss' first book was rejected by twenty-seven publishers before it was finally accepted? Aren't you glad Dr. Seuss (his real name was Theodore Seuss Geisel) didn't quit after number twenty-six? And then there is the popular *Chicken Soup for the Soul®* book series in which more than sixty million books have been sold in North America alone. Nevertheless, did you know that thirty-three publishers turned down the first book? That's right—thirty-three! No doubt, millions of readers are happy Jack Canfield and Victor Hansen didn't just give up.

Today there are powerful businesses which began in a crowded garage or once precariously teetered on bankruptcy. Many inventions that we now regularly use were previously laughed at or ignored. As a matter of fact, there was a time when every great invention, business, building, or ministry that we see today did not exist.

How about you? Are you using what you have? More importantly, are you using what you have for the glory of God? You see, doing what God wants us to do will always require a step of faith. You may feel entirely inadequate. But even though we may feel inadequate, the God we serve remains entirely adequate. Besides, it's nice to remember that some of the most spectacular feats have been accomplished by folks with a small safety pin and a little strand of fishing line.

Prayer: *Heavenly Father, help me to use whatever I have for Your glory. Amen.*

ALL THINGS ARE POSSIBLE
Scripture Reading: Mark 11:20-26

My brother spotted the large-racked buck, big doe, and a decent eight-pointer out in the middle of an open field. The snow was deep on that stormy December afternoon. And, to my brother (who would die in a car accident a few months later), the huge fourteen-pointer and the whitetails with him must have seemed unapproachable. Anyway, that's the only way I can explain his choice not to pursue this exceptional trio.

The flurries were heavy as I cut a path up the steep hill and then onto the tree-covered ridge which was above and behind the field where the three deer were. Walking out a point—I stopped. I could hear my brother yelling from the busy highway below, "Turn around! Turn around!"

As I turned, my eye caught site of the massive-racked fourteen-pointer charging up the hill some fifty to sixty yards behind me. I quickly pulled back my thirty-pound recurve and launched the arrow with an arc that resembled that of an English longbowman in battle. Although I never should have shot, the excitement proved too much.

Now, as you might have guessed, I missed that monster buck (which thirty plus years later still remains the largest I've ever seen). Nevertheless, just the fact that as a fourteen-year-old boy I got closer than most hunters still serves as a lasting source of encouragement. Yes, some things are worth trying—even when it may seem entirely useless to do so.

How much more should we attempt or ask for the impossible when serving the Lord? Jesus even encouraged His followers to exercise faith by saying, "Everything is possible for him who believes" (Mark 9:23b). And again, "All things are possible with God" (Mark 10:27b).

Friend, let's trust God for the impossible! Let's step out in faith! After all, "Without faith it is impossible to please God, because anyone who comes to him must believe that he exists and that he rewards those who earnestly seek him" (Hebrews 11:6).

Prayer: Lord Jesus, help me to believe You for the impossible! I ask this in Jesus' name. Amen.

THREE LEGS
Scripture Reading: Matthew 18:1-9

Andy was "special"—he had three legs. However, he wasn't born that way. Andy's lifestyle-change took place when many would have considered him to be middle-aged.

It happened one evening in a Wisconsin wood while he was in hot pursuit of a raccoon. Andy climbed a tree which was hanging out over a steep hillside. Then, attempting to turn around on a limb, he fell. All in all, Andy dropped some thirty feet. He broke one of his legs which eventually had to be amputated.

You see, Andy was a purebred bluetick coonhound. For the most part, he had always been a "silent trailer"—meaning that he limited his voice on the trail. Indeed, Andy surprised a lot of raccoon. However, after his accident this all changed.

Andy was frequently allowed the privilege of a solitary run (he was physically unable to handle much more than this). In the course of time, Andy converted. Out of necessity he became an "open trailer." This older dog somehow learned that in order to put a coon up a tree, he had to break his silence. Instead of speed, he started depending on the sound of his voice. Yes, to get what he wanted required change. The fact is, if a three-legged coonhound can recognize the need for change, so should we!

More importantly, Jesus told His disciples that change was not only possible, it was actually a prerequisite for getting a foot in heaven. He firmly stated, "I tell you the truth, unless you change and become like little children, you will never enter the kingdom of heaven" (Matthew 18:3). To be a follower of Jesus Christ requires change. Have you changed? With God's help it is possible for anyone to change.

Prayer: Lord God, keep changing me until I reflect Christ. Amen.

A SECRET MEANT TO BE SHARED
Scripture Reading: Mark 8:34-38

Jim Grassi is the type of person with which any angler would enjoy spending time. Not only is he a down-to-earth sort of guy, but as an international fishing instructor, Jim has fished from A to Z (Alaska to New Zealand). Grassi knows his stuff and each year continues to teach literally thousands of men, woman, girls, and boys how to successfully catch fish.

But even more importantly, Grassi is dedicated to sharing the Good News of Jesus Christ with others. He does this through fishing ministries, television, radio, and writing. In one of his books, Jim Grassi writes, "I think it is amazing to witness how excited fishermen can become when they find a new lure or product that creates excitement with the fish. They tell everyone they meet about the 'good news' of their product discovery and how it is making an impact on the fishery." (Jim Grassi, Promising Waters (Eugene: Harvest House, 1996), 76.)

How much more should we be excited about being able to share with others what simple, childlike faith in Jesus Christ can do. Not only is it possible to be forgiven for the failures of the past, but a genuine believer can also face the future with great confidence. As the apostle Paul (who previously had been a persecutor of the Church) publicly announced, "I am not ashamed of the gospel, because it is the power of God for the salvation of everyone who believes: first for the Jew, then for the Gentile" (Romans 1:16). No lure can compare with Christ! Let's share His great love with others!

Prayer: *Lord God, help me to not be afraid to share the Good News! I ask this in Jesus' Name. Amen.*

CONFESSIONS OF A POACHER
Scripture Reading: Psalm 51

Stepping out of the county courthouse, my eye caught something suspicious. There, next to the car, stood a stranger examining the deer tied to my trunk. A troubling thought quickly surfaced, "What if it's the game warden?"

You see, the same whitetail I was transporting with an archery tag on its leg had actually been shot with a twenty-two caliber rifle the day before. And the reason for coming to the courthouse was a way to cover up my wrongdoing. Having misplaced a portion of my archery license, I needed a duplicate. Now, with a replacement license in hand, the deer could be "legally" registered. However, the sight of this middle-aged man (who was evidently not a warden after all) pricked my already guilty conscience. The words of the wisdom writer rang true, "The wicked man flees though no one pursues" (Proverbs 28:1a).

Sadly, this was not the first, nor would it be the last, deer I poached. And, although many years have now passed since that incident took place, it's still hard to believe I could be so brazen.

Sin is covered in a lot of ways in our day. Sometimes it's the worker who calls in sick when he or she is not, the taxpayer who purposely fails to record extra income on their return or the hunter who inappropriately fills that tag of a hunting companion.

Whatever the case may be, the fact is nothing is hidden from God's eyes. The Bible says, "The eyes of the Lord are everywhere, keeping watch on the wicked and the good" (Proverbs 15:3). King David asked, "Where can I go from your Spirit? Where can I flee from your presence?" (Psalm 139:7) Indeed, nothing gets past God. He sees all! He hears all! He knows all!

But the good news is God is able to forgive *all* sin.

Even a murderer (such as King David) found grace in God's eyes.

Now, the fact is the Lord still has a lot of work to do in my life. I'm not perfect, but I am forgiven. And, if the Lord was willing to forgive me for a multitude of sins, He will also forgive you!

Prayer: *Lord God, thank You for the blood of Christ that covers our sins. Thank You for removing my transgressions "as far as the east is from the west" (Psalm 103:12a). Be honored in my life this day. In Jesus' name. Amen.*

WHERE'S THAT POINTER POINTING?
Scripture Reading: Romans 1:18-23

He froze motionless next to a clump of long, brown grass. This liver-and-white German short-haired pointer was locked on a ring-necked rooster. His right front paw was raised and his excited nose stretched forward. The pheasant with its spectacular plumage was crouched and poised to explode for better cover. What a sight!

The dog had been a gift from a family friend and the pheasant was one of hundreds I had raised and then released as part of a high school agriculture class project. Decades later this first observance of dog on point still remains a magnificent memory.

But just where was that pointer pointing? There are those who would argue that such a sight simply reveals specific characteristics or traits which have developed due to evolution or smart selective breeding.

However, according to the Bible such beauty and design must eventually be traced back to the invisible God who created all things. Indeed, as the apostle Paul reminded his readers in Rome, "For since the creation of the world God's invisible qualities— his eternal power and divine nature—have been clearly seen, being understood from what has been made, so that men are without excuse" (Romans 1:20). The fact is, God has left His invisible fingerprints all over His creation and every person in his or her heart of hearts knows this to be true.

So, where was that pointer pointing? The exact same place that the brightly-colored rooster pheasant was pointing—towards the invisible God who made all creatures great and small!

Prayer: *Lord, may my life point people to You. I ask this in Jesus' Name. Amen.*

THE DEVIL'S TACKLE BOX
Scripture Reading: Luke 4:1-13

I'm convinced the devil has a tackle box. Now I realize he doesn't have some sort of metal or plastic container with trays inside. However, he has a collection of things which he uses in order to entice and catch souls. He knows full well what we humans are most likely to sink our teeth into—and he does not practice catch and release. Indeed, the devil not only knows what type of lure to pick from his giant tackle box, but he also knows how to present the bait as well as when to set the hook. He's an expert at his trade, and no wonder, he has had thousands of years to practice.

Experienced anglers have their favorite spoons, spinners, flies, or plugs. And, apparently the enemy of our soul has his. When Jesus was led by the Holy Spirit into the desert and was "tempted by the devil" (Luke 4:2), we humans received an important glimpse into our enemy's tackle box.

For example, when Jesus was hungry, the devil tried to use basic physical hunger. In another attempt, the enemy took Christ to a high place and offered Him great honor and instant power for a seemingly small price. But perhaps most surprising is that the enemy incorporated holy and sacred things in order to tempt Christ. He used the "holy city" and "the temple" (Matthew 4:5), as well as the sacred Scriptures and the reality of angels (see Matthew 4:5; Luke 4:10).

Nevertheless, in each instance Jesus avoided the devil's barbed hook by quoting the Bible. And, if we want to avoid being on Satan's stringer we must do the same.

Prayer: Lord God, give me a heart to obey Your word. I ask this in Jesus' Name. Amen.

THINGS ARE NOT ALWAYS AS THEY APPEAR
Scripture Reading: Hebrews 13:1-6

It was just before 6:00 am when I pulled my twenty-plus-year-old car into the public hunting ground parking area. The big old Chevrolet I was driving had a rapidly rotting cloth roof and a rusting yellow body. It was known by family and friends as "The Bruised Banana." When I returned a couple of hours later from my early morning bow hunt I was surprised to find an orange card placed on the windshield. The card was signed by a deputy sheriff and said, "Abandoned Vehicle."

Now I don't know if the car's engine was still warm when the deputy tagged it as "abandoned." Nevertheless, I do know that I had no intention of abandoning the old beater. When I later called the sheriff's office to find out what I should do, I was told to just ignore the "Abandoned Vehicle" card. I also jokingly remarked to the sheriff's dispatcher, "You kind of hurt my feelings!"

Even so, it was understandable how the deputy—judging by mere appearance of my car—could conclude that it had been "abandoned." But, we know that things are not always as they appear.

The same is also the case when we consider some of the people who lived in Bible times. Sometimes the circumstances that surrounded their lives seemed to say they were abandoned by God. For example, in the Old Testament book of Genesis we read how Joseph was sold into slavery by his own brothers and ended up in a foreign land as a servant to an Egyptian named Potiphar. It certainly would have appeared that God had abandoned him. Yet, the Scriptures tell us, "The Lord was with Joseph and he prospered, and he lived in the house of his Egyptian master" (Genesis 39:2).

And later, when he was falsely accused by Potiphar's wife and thrown in jail it would have seemed as though God had split the scene. But again the Bible tells us, "The Lord was with Joseph and gave him success in whatever he did" (Genesis 39:23b). Of course, Joseph later rose to a place of great prominence in Egypt.

In the New Testament the Apostle Paul experienced great suffering as he declared the Good News of Jesus Christ. Paul was falsely imprisoned, whipped, beaten, was stoned and left for dead, faced danger, as well as hunger and thirst (see 2 Corinthians 11:21-29). Many times it would have seemed as if Paul was abandoned by the Lord. But despite all that Paul and his companions went through, God remained faithful. Paul told the Christians at Corinth, "We are hard pressed on every side, but not crushed; perplexed, but not in despair; persecuted, but not abandoned" (2 Corinthians 4:8-9).

Furthermore, when Jesus commissioned His disciples to proclaim the Good News, He knew that they would be rejected and experience various trials. There would be times when it would appear they had been abandoned. In fact, according to tradition most of His close followers were eventually put to death. He knew He was sending them out into a hostile and cruel world. But, just before He ascended to heaven Jesus promised his disciples, "Surely I am with you always, to the very end of the age" (Matthew 28:20).

The truth is that even though we may be abandoned by close friends and even family members—God will never abandon His own. Regardless of what the circumstances say, God will not forsake His children. Indeed, God has clearly promised, "Never will I leave you; never will I forsake you" (Hebrews 13:5b). Friend, God will never abandon you.

Prayer: *Lord, thank You for not abandoning me. Amen.*

THE NORTH AMERICAN HUNTER: AN ENDANGERED SPECIES? (PART I)
Scripture Reading: Genesis 1:26-31

The extensive teaching of evolution has been partially responsible for a distorted distinction between humans and animals. Because of evolution, animals and humans alike are being viewed very differently from just decades ago.

Today in most science classes, this theory is being eloquently preached on a regular basis. Not only does evolution place humans and other creatures on a similar plateau, but evolution ultimately undermines the unique worth humans have been assigned in the biblical record. The Bible makes it clear that humans are distinct from the rest of creation because they are made in the "image of God" (Genesis 1:27).

Prayer: *Father, thank You for sharing Your creation with us. Help me to realize the unique value of all creation and to see hunters and non-hunters as having all been made in Your image. I ask this in the name of Jesus. Amen.*

THE NORTH AMERICAN HUNTER: AN ENDANGERED SPECIES? (PART II)
Scripture Reading: Revelation 20:11-15

Why are many people currently opposed to hunting? The answers to such a question would probably be too numerous to tabulate. But a primary reason for the anti-hunter attitude that exists today can be traced to the increasing influence of Eastern thought on our society.

Religions such as Buddhism and Hinduism have made the concept of coming back to life in different forms very popular. This idea, which is known as "reincarnation", is presently being propagated through the New Age movement. Let's face it, even taking the life of a rat is difficult if there remains the remote possibility it was a relative of which you were previously fond.

But the Judeo-Christian principles upon which this country was primarily founded do not teach reincarnation. In fact, they teach just the opposite. God's Word makes it clear we have one life. In the New Testament book of Hebrews the Bible tells us, "Man is destined to die once, and after that to face judgment" (Hebrews 9:27).

Prayer: *Heavenly Father, thank You that we can "know you, the only true God, and Jesus Christ, whom you have sent" (John 17:3). Help me to live this one life for Your glory. In Jesus' name. Amen.*

HOW'S YOUR FISHING FORM?
Scripture Reading: Luke 11:1-3

Time and again, my line floated undisturbed past a partially submerged snag. It was the same place where earlier I had felt the solid tug of a good trout on my fly rod.

Suddenly, it struck me what was wrong. I had been so busy trying to make the right presentation that I hadn't noticed my fly was missing. Since the previous strike, I had been fishing without a hook!

Unfortunately, many well-meaning church people are doing something similar. Although they may be sincere and appear to others as having it all together, in reality they are merely going through the motions. Like an egg shell drained of its contents, so these appear outwardly to have something within—but inside they are empty. They have what Paul referred to in the New Testament as "a form of godliness" (2 Timothy 3:5).

The truth of the matter is a person can be baptized, confirmed, join the organized church, and even read the Bible on a regular basis. Nevertheless, if that individual has never been "born again" (John 3:3), his or her religion is empty. Such individuals are like artificial flowers. They outwardly look like the real thing, but there is no life within. They are disconnected like a branch that has been severed from the tree. Such hypocrites are like clouds that have no rain within. As the Apostle Paul pointed out to the Christians in Rome, "if anyone does not have the Spirit of Christ, he does not belong to Christ" (Romans 8:9). However, the good news is that by simple faith in Jesus Christ, we can receive the promise of the Holy Spirit.

Prayer: *Lord, thank You for making it possible to live the Christian life by granting the gift of Your Holy Spirit. Amen.*

PERSISTENCE PAYS OFF
Scripture Reading: Luke 18:1-8

Deer hunting is one area where the statement "persistence pays off" can really be put to the test. It takes persistence to continue to crawl out of bed each morning in order to stumble to your stand before daylight. It takes persistence to sit for hours shivering for hours in the rain or snow without catching so much as even a glimpse of a deer.

Even so, persistence in deer hunting is frequently found to pay off in the long run. Frequently, it is the final drive of the day or the last minute in the stand that ends up making the difference. The fact is, each year some of the biggest bucks are harvested after many hunters have hung it up for the season.

Unfortunately many of us who are so persistent when it comes to deer hunting are easily persuaded to give it up in the spiritual realm. This is especially sad when we realize that although the odds are good that our persistence will pay off when it comes to deer hunting—there are still no guarantees.

However, this is not the case in the spiritual realm. In the spiritual realm, the believer has been given promises to help make it easier to continue on. We have a book filled with guarantees for those who persevere. This book is called the Bible.

Prayer: *Heavenly Father, thank You for all the promises we have in Christ. Help me to be persistent, especially in the area of prayer. I ask this in Jesus' name. Amen.*

BARNYARD BUCK
Scripture Reading: 1 Kings 19:1-18

I parked my car next to a shed and proceeded up the hill between the new church building being erected and the weed-filled barnyard. When I returned two hours later, it seemed as if the buck waited for an opportune time before busting out of the dried weeds. Although he was less than fifty feet away, he caught me so off guard I almost dropped my rifle. When I did finally recover from my juggling act, the buck was moving so fast, and I was so shaken up, he had little to worry about. I did get off a few shots as he continued to shrink in my open sights, but to no avail.

The truth of the matter is, after opening day, a person's liable to find deer just about anywhere—next to buildings, in a small patch of grass, or even in a barnyard. The buck you're after is probably still out there, but not where you would expect to find him.

So, it often is with God. He is sometimes in things and at places we don't expect. In today's Scripture reading, we learn that Elijah saw a powerful wind, an earthquake, and a fire. However, God was not in these. Instead, God was in something far less magnificent. You see, Elijah had often observed God working in dramatic ways. Previously, he witnessed a boy being raised from the dead (1 Kings 17:22), fire fall from heaven (1 Kings 18:38), and a torrential downpour ending three-and-a-half years of drought (1 Kings 18:45).

We also tend to think that God should always use the big, flashy things to reveal His presence. We expect Him to speak to us like the great Oz spoke to Dorothy and her friends in *The Wizard of Oz*. But God isn't as predictable as a Hollywood movie script. He often uses a child, a circumstance, or even a familiar portion of Scripture. What really matters is not how God chooses to communicate, but that we respond in the right way when He does.

Prayer: Father, help me to be alert and to respond when You speak. May I see You in even the ordinary experiences of life. In Jesus' name. Amen.

JUST FLOAT AND FISH
Scripture Reading: Luke 14:25-35

    My wife, Beth, and I had been married about six months when we had a chance to get away for Memorial Day weekend. Weekends off are an especially rare commodity for pastors. And, because Beth was working a full-time job during the week—and in the pastorate things get more hectic as the weekend approaches—we were looking forward to a relaxing time together.
    I had an idea! Why not take my folks' ten-foot flat bottom boat down the Wisconsin river? We could take our dog Nameless (that was the only name we could agree on), a couple of sleeping bags, fishing poles, and some plastic to put under our sleeping bags. I would fast and seek God's guidance for the future and Beth would take some food for herself. If I decided to eat, I could always catch a fish. I had heard that the Wisconsin flowed at a certain speed. So, I calculated that we could simply sit back, float, fish, and read. It even sounded rather romantic!
    So, I parked my old station wagon in a little town some forty-seven miles downstream. Having gotten started late on Saturday, we only made it a few miles on the river before it got dark. However, we felt fortunate to find a large sandbar about three-quarters of an acre in size that we had all to ourselves. Despite not being able to get a fire started due to damp wood and our late start, this was still going to be a great weekend!
    But, that night intoxicated campers on both sides of the river kept us up, our dog discovered the moon at three in the morning, and the temperature plummeted to almost freezing.
    Then things started taking a turn for the worse. At daylight we discovered that our rather large sandbar had shrunk to a circle of about twenty-five feet in diameter. During the night they had raised the water level by

opening the gates on the dam upstream. By the grace of God, we happened to be in that circle—the only part of the sandbar not underwater!

It started raining. We got in the boat. Nevertheless, it seemed that the wind was blowing harder upstream than the current was flowing down. We were wet and cold. I had a splitting headache and was hungry! I couldn't catch a fish—and with everything being drenched by the rain, I wouldn't have been able to cook one if I had. So, my wife shared her food ration. Now there were two half-hungry, cranky people instead of just one. We were going home. We had had enough of this river!

That day I rowed over forty miles. When it became dark and I kept rowing onto sandbars, I pulled my wife and our young dog in the boat down the last three miles of the river. This was one Memorial Day weekend we would always remember.

Of course the real problem was not the river, it was not being prepared for what the journey might hold. However, Jesus Christ never painted any unrealistic pictures for his followers. He wanted them to be prepared. For example, He said, "If they persecuted me, they will persecute you also" (John 15:20b). And again, "Any of you who does not give up everything he has cannot be my disciple" (Luke 14:33). Are you prepared to follow Christ? It can be rough, but it is worth it!

Prayer: *Lord, help me to faithfully run the race You have marked out for me. In Jesus' name. Amen.*

TRAPPED
Scripture Reading: Galatians 6:1-5

Have you ever been trapped? Not long ago I found myself trapped in Des Moines, Iowa. Now there were no chains, ropes, or even locked doors that kept me confined. No one was physically restraining me. Nevertheless, for a short period of time I could not, or rather would not leave my location.

This little episode I'm talking about took place in a convention center where a large deer hunting expo was being held. There were literally thousands of people within shouting distance. Nevertheless, most of these people never knew about my predicament—and for this I am thankful!

My problem started shortly after lunch. I needed to go to the bathroom. So, seeing a restroom not far from where I had just finished eating—I hurried into a stall and sat down. I could hear the normal sounds one hears in this kind of bathroom such as: the slamming of bathroom stall doors, flushing toilets, water running in the sink, etc.

However, after a few minutes my eye caught a glance of someone through the crack in the bathroom stall door. I could see an individual standing at the wash sink fixing their waist-length blonde hair in the mirror. I thought, "That guy sure has long blonde hair." After a few moments the person left, but I continued silently musing to myself, "I like long hair, but a man having hair that long is a little ridiculous. Why—from behind that guy looks more like a wom . . . ."

Suddenly, I had this really bad feeling. I realized—and then said under my breath, "OH NO! I'M SITTING IN THE WOMEN'S BATHROOM!"

I looked down at my "man" shoes which were certainly visible from outside the stall—and cringed. I listened closely, and when things got quiet at the sink I made a fast break for the doorway. As I came out and took a quick left I heard someone over my right shoulder say, "Hey, that guy just came out of the women's bathroom!" I kept walking and never looked back!

Now it's a terrible (and sometimes even an embarrassing) thing to be trapped. But the fact is, many in our culture (even a percentage of professing Christians) are currently trapped in some sort of sinful behavior. Countless people have been captured by alcohol, prescription drugs, pornography, or a compulsion to gamble. Millions more are controlled by an addiction for food, or by eating disorders like anorexia or bolemia. Furthermore, great numbers continue to live in bondage to credit card and other types of financial debt. Wealthy King Solomon warned, "The borrower is servant to the lender" (Proverbs 22:7b).

Being trapped in sin is far more serious than simply getting stuck in the wrong bathroom. Jesus said, "Everyone who sins is a slave to sin" (John 8:34). The Lord warned Ezekiel, "The soul who sins is the one who will die" (Ezekiel 18:4b). Indeed, being trapped in sin results in bondage and even death.

The good news is we don't have to live in bondage. We don't have to stay trapped. Jesus Christ Himself said, "So if the Son sets you free, you will be free indeed" (John 8:36). Friend, are you trapped? Christ can and will set you free.

Prayer: *Heavenly Father, thank You for Your perfect and complete deliverance. Keep me from stepping into the enemy's snares. I ask this in Jesus' name. Amen.*

LITTLE WINDOWS OF OPPORTUNITY
Scripture Reading: Ephesians 5:15-21

From the first flutter of feathers as a grouse breaks forth from the brush, until it disappears through the trees offers even the best bird hunter only a tiny window of opportunity. Indeed, many a ruffed grouse has escaped a shotgun pattern by relying upon its exceptional speed and remarkable ability to dodge through branches. Although I have enjoyed some success at bringing down grouse—many more times I have totally missed the moment of opportunity. Far too often the grouse has been gone even before the shotgun made it to my shoulder.

A similar thing happens when it comes to the opportunities God gives us in this life. He grants each of us the privilege to do His will. I know that I have missed many of these God-ordered golden opportunities. How about you? Have you been missing your God granted chances?

Paul told the believers in Ephesus, "Be very careful, then, how you live—not as unwise but as wise, making the most of every opportunity, because the days are evil" (Ephesians 5:15-16). And, to the church in Galatia Paul pointed out the need for his readers to be taking advantage of the opportunities to help both unbelievers and believers. He urged, "Therefore, as we have opportunity, let us do good to all people, especially to those who belong to the family of believers" (Galatians 6:10). Today let's be looking for those windows of opportunity regardless of how small or large they may be.

Prayer: *Heavenly Father, help me to use the time You have given me for Your glory. Help me to spot the opportunities You want me to seize. I ask this in the name of Your Son, Jesus. Amen.*

Devotions for Hunters & Anglers

THE ANTLERED DOE
Scripture Reading: 1 Samuel 16:1-13

Where I grew up, deer hunting was, and still is, an important part of the culture. Each year a person from the local newspaper would walk over to the police station where many deer were brought to be registered. This same individual would then take a picture of someone who brought in a nice buck and then include it in an article about that year's hunt.

In 1971, at the age of fourteen, a photo of me standing next to a deer that had one antler ended up on the paper's front page. At first glance, it would simply appear that some young fellow bagged a buck that had half a rack.

Nevertheless, things aren't always as they appear. The caption below the photo stated, "Tom Rakow, a young hunter, registered this antlered doe at the police station last week. One of the antlers had been broken off and the one remaining was still in velvet." Indeed, things aren't always as they appear.

Although the reporter who had come to the police station and taken the picture stated that one antler had been broken off, this was not completely true. Actually, the doe had only grown the one velvet-covered fork. In addition, by looking at the photo in the paper it would seem reasonable to assume that the person next to the pickup truck's endgate with his hand on the deer's neck was the one who had harvested this whitetail oddity.

However, again things are not always as they appear. While it was true that it was my tag on the deer's leg, my dad was really the one who had bagged this pseudo buck.

When you come to think of it, there are a lot of things in this world that aren't always as they appear. Take for example the person who outwardly looks like they have everything (money, fame, looks, etc.). More often than not, this same individual is inwardly empty and privately miserable.

Then there is the criminal caught red-handed, but who gets off the hook due to some minor legal technicality. From a strictly human viewpoint, it appears they have gotten away with it. But again, things aren't always as they appear.

According to the Bible, "There is nothing hidden that will not be disclosed, and nothing concealed that will not be known or brought out into the open" (Luke 8:17). As the Apostle Paul wrote the Christians in Galatia, "Do not be deceived: God cannot be mocked. A man reaps what he sows" (Galatians 6:7).

I am reminded of a thief I heard about on the east coast who burglarized a house. For all practical purposes, it appeared that it was a clean getaway. Except, that is, for one telling mistake. When he backed out of the driveway, he backed into a snowbank. He drove away, but left the imprint of his license in the snow. The license plate was traced down, and he was locked up. Yes, this crook learned the hard way that things aren't always as they appear!

The Bible makes it clear that not everyone who professes to know Christ truly does. Jesus not only warned of false prophets who would appear to be one thing, but were really another (see Matthew 7:15), He also stated, "Not everyone who says to me, 'Lord, Lord,' will enter the kingdom of heaven, but only he who does the will of my Father who is in heaven" (Matthew 7:21). In fact, Jesus went on to say, "Many will say to me on that day, 'Lord, Lord, did we not prophesy in your name, and in your name drive out demons and perform many miracles?' Then I will tell them plainly, 'I never knew you. Away from me, you evildoers!'" (Matthew 7:22-23). You see, the Lord sees things as they are, not merely as they appear.

The good news is that God knows if we belong to

Him. As Paul told a young preacher named Timothy, "'The Lord knows those who are his,' and, 'Everyone who confesses the name of the Lord must turn away from wickedness'" (2 Timothy 2:19).

All who know Christ have something wonderful to look forward to. John stated, "Dear friends, now we are children of God, and what we will be has not yet been made known. But we know that when he appears, we shall be like him, for we shall see him as he is" (1 John 3:2).

Prayer: Lord, help me to see things from Your perspective. In Christ's name. Amen.

DOES GOD CARE ABOUT ANIMALS AND BIRDS?
Scripture Reading: Luke 12:22-34

The first book of the Bible tells how God went to all the trouble of preserving animals and birds from the flood in Noah's day by directing an ark to be built (Genesis 6-9). We also find in the New Testament that even such an insignificant creature as a little sparrow is important. Jesus told his disciples, "Are not five sparrows sold for two pennies? Yet not one of them is forgotten by God" (Luke 12:6).

It's interesting that, from early on, God gave the Israelites specific guidelines for how animals and birds were to be treated. These directives included such things as rest on the Sabbath (Exodus 20:10; 23:12; Deuteronomy 5:14), the way work was to be accomplished (Deuteronomy 22:10; 25:4), provisions of food to be left for wild animals (Exodus 23:10-11; Leviticus 25:6-7), and proper treatment of a bird with her young (Deuteronomy 22:6-7). The book of Proverbs made it clear that the way a man treated his animal was a reflection upon his true moral character, "A righteous man cares for the needs of his animal, but the kindest acts of the wicked are cruel" (Proverbs 12:10). Even the handling and use of game that had been harvested received comment. The inspired Scriptures state, "The lazy man does not roast his game, but the diligent man prizes his possessions" (Proverbs 12:27).

Although Jesus stated that His disciples were "worth more than many sparrows" (Luke 12:7) and that a man's value is greater than that of a sheep's (Matthew 12:12), He never released humans from their responsibility of proper stewardship over His creatures. God desires that those who have been made in His own image should govern His creation appropriately. It only stands to reason that the way to have a right relationship with creation is by first having a right relationship with the Creator.

Prayer: Lord God, thank You for providing what is necessary in this world. Help me to hunt in a way that is honorable to You. I ask this in Jesus' name. Amen.

ONE-EYED
Scripture Reading: Luke 11:33-36

After the mishap, we found him laying alone in a dark hay mow. Although it took place well over three decades ago—I still remember the instant my dad shined the light on his face. Through the darkness a single eye reflected back, and where the other eye should have been—blood glistened from an empty socket.

Indeed, by human standards he was handicapped. Furthermore, besides having an untraceable family tree, he was also given a rather bland name which was virtually void of creativity.

Nevertheless, he sure knew how to hunt! Yes, Rover, my one-eyed collie cross who lost his left eye after being hit by a car was quite a squirrel dog.

Now admittedly, for many, the thought of fresh squirrel pie might not conjure up much of an appetite. "After all," someone might ask, "isn't the squirrel really a member of the rodent family?" Even so, in the hardwood covered hills where I grew up, eating squirrel was much more than a treat or tradition, it was a lifestyle. A good squirrel dog was truly appreciated and Rover was a good squirrel dog.

Mick, my older teenage brother (now deceased) came to the conclusion that the key to Rover's hunting success had to do with his having only one eye. He figured having only one eye prevented him from being distracted by anything else. In hindsight, I think my brother was right. When it came to chasing squirrels, Rover knew how to focus.

The fact is we all focus on something. We either live for the glory, gusto, or gold of this world which is guaranteed to pass away or, as the Apostle Paul explained to the Christians in Corinth, "We fix our eyes not on what is seen, but on what is unseen. For what is seen is temporary, but what is unseen is eternal" (2 Corinthians 4:18).

In the Bible, eyes are frequently viewed as instruments that either determine or reveal a person's true moral direction and character. No doubt about it, where our physical and spiritual eyes are focused can make all the difference. Jesus warned His listeners, "If your right eye causes you to sin, gouge it out and throw it away. It is better for you to lose one part of your body than for your whole body to go into hell" (Matthew 5:29). And again, Jesus stated, "Your eye is the lamp of your body. When your eyes are good, your whole body also is full of light. But when they are bad, your body also is full of darkness" (Luke 11:34).

Yes, God holds us responsible for what we focus on. If a one-eyed dog named Rover can keep his focus when chasing squirrels—we should also have enough foresight to keep our eyes fixed on the Lord. As the writer of the book of Hebrews charged the Jewish believers of his day, "Let us fix our eyes on Jesus, the author and perfecter of our faith, who for the joy set before him endured the cross, scorning its shame, and sat down at the right hand of the throne of God" (Hebrews 12:2).

Prayer: Lord, keep my eyes fixed on You. May others fix their gaze in Your direction as well. I ask this in Jesus' name. Amen.

LUCKY
Scripture Reading: Numbers 21:4-9

Several years ago I was fishing with my wife and four young daughters alongside a little lake a couple miles from home. It was a beautiful June afternoon and the kids were keeping me busy either putting on night crawlers, taking off fish, reeling in lines, or casting them back out. I didn't even attempt to fish myself—that is until my wife decided it was time to take our youngest daughter back home. I was going to use her pole until one of my daughters protested, "I want to use mom's big pole!"

"Fine," I said, "I'll just use your little Snoopy pole" (a short kid's pole with a Snoopy sticker).

Minutes later I landed a six-and-a-half pound large mouth bass. The fish was almost as long as the little Snoopy pole itself. Suddenly, everyone wanted to use the "lucky" Snoopy pole. In their young minds the explanation for dad suddenly catching this lunker had to do with the particular pole he was using.

Now we all know that superstition or a belief in lucky objects is not just confined to children. Even many adults carry their lucky charms or go through some religious ritual in hopes of controlling the future. Indeed, we humans have a tendency to chalk up good fortune and sometimes even bad fortune to a particular object, arrangement of objects, or some habitual behavior. In fact, today there are literally hundreds if not thousands of businesses and websites that either cater to, or capitalize upon, this concept we call "good luck."

But such behavior or belief systems are not new with our culture. Attempts to obtain some sort of "good luck" or favorable outcome can actually be traced back thousands of years. We know that on certain occasions people in Bible times were prone to begin admiring, honoring, or even worshiping things that God had used to accomplish the miraculous.

We could certainly point to an ephod made by Gideon (see Judges 8:22-27) or a sacred chest called the "ark of the covenant" (see 1 Samuel 4:1-11). Nevertheless, one of the clearest examples found in Scripture would have to be the bronze serpent.

In the book of Numbers we are told that the children of Israel sinned and began speaking against God and His servant Moses. We are told, "The Lord sent venomous snakes among them; they bit the people and many Israelites died" (Numbers 21:6). As a result they cried out to Moses and asked him to pray on their behalf that the Lord would take the snakes away. Instead of taking the snakes away the Lord instructed Moses to make a serpent out of bronze. The Lord promised when anyone was bitten if they looked at the bronze serpent they would live. When the Israelites did this, they found the Lord's promise to be true.

However, as the years passed something strange happened. Instead of honoring God, the Hebrew people began honoring and worshipping the bronze snake that the Lord had used to accomplish this miracle. We are told that King Hezekiah "broke into pieces the bronze snake Moses had made, for up to that time the Israelites had been burning incense to it. (It was called Nehushtan.)" (2 Kings 18:4b)

In a similar fashion, we Christians can also become more enamored with the things the Lord has used in our lives rather than with the Lord Himself. For example, God may have used a particular hymn, ministry, or preacher to accomplish something great in our life. Yet, we can become so focused upon this event or experience of the past that we fail to see God at work in the present. As a result we can start to think God must use only a particular style of music, a specific kind of ministry, or a certain type of preaching. But God is not limited to always using the same things to accomplish His work. Let's not depend upon luck—let's depend upon the Lord!

Prayer: *Father, help me to be open to the new things You want to do. Keep me from becoming so attached to the things You have used in the past that I miss what You are doing in the present. I ask this for Your name's sake. Amen.*

LITTLE THINGS MEAN A LOT
Scripture Reading: Luke 17:1-10

Little things are often overlooked, but little things can, and often do, make a BIG difference. Indeed, little things mean a lot!

For example, a little pill for high blood pressure can help prevent a major stroke and even death. On the other hand, a microscopic virus or tiny infection can bring down even the healthiest and heartiest of humans.

The postage stamp, although small in size, when placed on an envelope can cause a letter to be carried to a destination literally thousands of miles away. However, without that little postage stamp even the most important document won't travel very far.

Certainly a single grain of sand on a highway won't stop a big semi-truck. Nevertheless, a grain of sand in the eye of the driver can keep both off the road.

These days one thin dime may not purchase much. Even so, that same coin can serve as a screwdriver in a pinch. Yes, sometimes a little dime can do what a hundred dollar bill can not.

Or, consider a simple safety pin. The lowly safety pin can prevent a person whose zipper has broke, or hem has unraveled from making an embarrassing fashion statement!

We know that a giant redwood tree is grown from a single small seed. Nevertheless, one little wooden match can burn down a great forest with millions of trees.

Miniature fish hooks have caught big fish. Yet, even small fish can be used in a magnificent way. I know a professional angler who won an important fishing tournament and received the $50,000 cash prize. He told me that none of his fish were really big, in fact they were kind of small, but together they averaged enough to make him the winner.

In the New Testament, Jesus Christ fed thousands with a boy's "five small barley loaves and two small fish" (John 6:9). Yes, the Lord can use little things to accomplish much.

We are often impressed with big stuff, but we shouldn't look down on what appears to be small or insignificant. When a man named Zerubbabel was involved in the rebuilding of the Jewish temple, some thought it was insignificant in comparison to the previous temple which had been destroyed. However, the Lord asked, "Who despises the day of small things?" (Zechariah 4:10). You see, when the Lord is involved in something—even if might seem to be a small thing—it can carry great significance.

With God's help we can all do something big—even if by the world's standards what we are doing seems rather small. There is an old saying that states, "Big doors often swing on small hinges." Look around. Are there some doors in need of hinges? Are there some small things that the Lord wants you to do? Remember, little things mean a lot—especially when the Lord of the universe is involved!

Prayer: *Heavenly Father, help me to be faithful in the little things You have called me to do. I ask this in Jesus' name. Amen.*

BUCK IN THE SHADOWS
Scripture Reading: Luke 16:19-31

He was grinding acorns between his teeth as he grazed his way within fifteen yards of the tree I was hunting from. I strained to see a shape. It was several minutes into legal shooting hours. However, the overcast sky and heavy foliage from the grove of oaks in which I was situated shut out what little daylight there was.

Then as I hoped, this unseen chewing, shadowy form moved even closer. Minutes passed. First, a hunk of the buck's polished rack became visible, then his outline. He moved within feet of the large limb on which I was perched. I partially pulled on the string of my recurve—and then waited. I thought, "Why not reduce the risk of a miss altogether? After all, within a matter of moments it'll be a sure thing." But then, suddenly, without warning, he turned, trotted into the tangled undergrowth, and was gone!

I hunted that buck hard for weeks. Every time I saw the heavy, long tracks he left behind, I was painfully reminded of having blown it. I had waited too long. In an attempt to reduce all risk, I had actually created risk. Indeed, I still regret having passed up that shot.

Even so, according to the Bible, some will pass up something far greater. Unfortunately, many will spend all of eternity reminded of the fact that they blew their biggest opportunity of all. Namely, their chance to gain eternal life. They may remember a sermon they heard, the witness of a friend, or even an entry in this devotional booklet. In any case, the Bible states that many will wait too long before they respond to the Good News of Jesus Christ. As a result they will spend eternity in the torments of hell.

On one occasion, Jesus Christ was asked, "Lord, are

only a few people going to be saved?" (Luke 13:23b)

He responded, "Make every effort to enter through the narrow door, because many, I tell you, will try to enter and will not be able to. Once the owner of the house gets up and closes the door, you will stand outside knocking and pleading, 'Sir, open the door for us.' But he will answer, 'I don't know you or where you come from'" (Luke 13:24-25). Yes, many will wait too long. Those who wait until tomorrow put themselves at great risk. For as the Bible says, "Now is the time of God's favor, now is the day of salvation" (2 Corinthians 6:2b). Tomorrow may be too late!

Prayer: *Heavenly Father, thank You that no one needs to go to hell because Your Son paid the price for our sin on the cross. Use me to win others to You. In Your name I pray. Amen.*

FALSE POINTING
Scripture Reading: 2 Corinthians 5:1-10

There is something special about watching a pointer quartering back and forth into the wind. But it's even more spectacular is to see that same dog go on point and suddenly turn into a living statue. However, sometimes a dog will false point. That is to say a dog will go on point because it caught a whiff of a bird—or saw something that looked like a bird—but no bird is present.

Sometimes we as Christians also do some false pointing. We may interpret some little event, or an open door as evidence of God's will for our life—but it ends up not working out. Those looking at our lives when this happens may be inclined to doubt God. However, the problem is not with God, but with our impatience and desire to walk by sight rather than by faith.

Jesus told some religious leaders who were asking him for a sign, "A wicked and adulterous generation looks for a miraculous sign, but none will be given it except the sign of Jonah" (Matthew 16:4a). The resurrection of Christ became a powerful sign to that generation—and still is today.

And, although God still performs miracles when He so chooses, He desires—and even requires—us to walk by faith. We are to trust Him even when there may be few if any visible proofs of His presence. As Paul told the Christians in Corinth, "We live by faith, not by sight" (2 Corinthians 5:7). Again, as the writer of Hebrews stated, "Without faith it is impossible to please God" (Hebrews 11:6a). Let's be careful not to "false point." Rather let us choose to continue to walk by faith.

Prayer: Lord, may my life consistently point people to You. I ask this in Jesus' name. Amen.

THE COAT
Scripture Reading: Isaiah 55:6-11

For more than half a century, my dad successfully hunted raccoon. Indeed, it's no exaggeration when I say that he spent literally thousands of nights under star-studded skies.

He not only had a passion for the solitude of a late night hunt, but also for the interruption of that same solitude with the sound of a hound either hot on a trail or barking at the tree.

I guess it's only natural that a houndsperson and their dog come to have a unique relationship. Although my dad seldom babied his hounds, he did love them. He took care of them. And we had good dogs. Dogs that were straight. By this I mean that they ran raccoon—and nothing else.

Even so, there were a few times when he would temporarily lose one. It didn't happen often, but it did happen. Usually it was on a windy night when the rattling of cornstalks hampered hearing them. Sometimes they were treeing on the other side of a steep hill or somewhere in a secluded brushy hollow.

When a dog was gone too long on a run, you could sense in Dad's voice both his confidence and concern. Confidence that the hound was on a raccoon and concern that the dog was either caught in a fence or perhaps some other hunter had picked up the dog.

On those rare occasions when a dog did have to be left behind until morning, my dad always did something before we left. Dad would take his jacket off and spread it out on the ground. If there was a cornfield nearby where we had initially parked the truck, he would take the coat in a couple of rows and make a comfortable nest. When Dad returned early the next morning, he would find the dog either curled up on the coat or still at the tree. Yes, Dad's hounds knew where they would find the one who loved them and would take care of them.

In a similar way, God has also left something behind for us as humans so that we can be reunited with our Master. He left it in the Bible. It's not a garment, but rather something far greater. Namely, a wide trail of prophetic passages. Information that has the power to convince and lead a person who is honestly searching for truth into a personal relationship with God's Son—the Lord Jesus Christ.

Indeed, God purposely provided the world with a sacred stream of futuristic truth—a brook of revelation regarding the One whom Hebrew prophets and priests longed to see. A river that continued to flow deeper and wider with the passing of each century until its final fulfillment in Christ.

You see, in our Bibles there exist literally scores of Scriptures which foretold such things as: where the Christ would be born (Micah 5:2), that the child's mother would be a virgin (Isaiah 7:14), as well as the murderous decision of Herod after Christ's birth to have all the baby boys in the vicinity of Bethlehem killed (Jeremiah 31:15).

In addition, the Old Testament writings also predicted the Messiah's ministry (Isaiah 61:1-2), abandonment by His disciples (Zechariah 13:7), casting of lots for Christ's clothes (Psalm 22:18), the piercing of His side with a spear (Zechariah 12:10), and the resurrection of His body (Psalm 16:8-11) just to name a few.

What it really comes down to is this: if a person is looking for someone who really cares for them, the answer is to be found in the Bible. Yes, the answer is found in the person of Jesus Christ who said regarding Himself, "The Son of Man came to seek and to save what was lost" (Luke 19:10). After all, if coonhounds know where to find their master—so should we!

Prayer: Heavenly Father, thank You for sending Your Son, Jesus Christ. Thank You for leaving such a wide trail down through the centuries. May others recognize that You are my Master. I ask this in Christ's name. Amen.

A KEEPER?
Scripture Reading: Matthew 3:1-12

Two men who were fishing on a Sunday morning were feeling guilty, especially since the fish weren't biting. Finally one said to the other, "I guess I should have stayed home and gone to church."

To which the other fisherman responded, "I couldn't have gone to church anyway! My wife's sick in bed."

Now we may laugh at that little story. However, even something as seemingly harmless as fishing (if not in proper balance) can ruin a relationship with the Lord and wreak havoc in a family.

The Bible tells us there is actually coming a time when God will deal with all of humanity similar to the way that an angler deals with his or her catch. He will determine what is worth keeping and what is not. In explaining the kingdom of heaven, Jesus compared it to "a net that was let down into the lake and caught all kinds of fish. When it was full, the fishermen pulled it up on the shore. Then they sat down and collected the good fish in baskets, but threw the bad away" (Matthew 13:47-48). The Lord then goes on to explain that this is a picture of what it will be like at the end of the age. He states, "The angels will come and separate the wicked from the righteous and throw them into the fiery furnace, where there will be weeping and gnashing of teeth" (Matthew 13:49-50).

Unfortunately, many in the organized church of today fail to realize that God can tell the difference between a person who has truly trusted Christ and a mere pretender. He knows what we are really like and if we truly belong to Him. As the Apostle Paul pointed out, "Nevertheless, God's solid foundation stands firm, sealed with this inscription: 'The Lord knows those who are his,' and, 'Everyone who confesses the name of the Lord must turn away from wickedness'" (2 Timothy 2:19).

Although a person's relationship with the Lord may not always be apparent to us, it is clear to Him. Yes, "the Lord knows those who are his."

God's word tells us there is coming a time when, "All the nations will be gathered before him, and he will separate the people one from another as a shepherd separates the sheep from the goats" (Matthew 25:32). Yes, the Lord is able to make a distinction. Jesus made it painfully clear that many people who have appeared to be serving Christ will eventually be exposed and, ultimately, rejected. In Matthew 7:22-23 He announced, "Many will say to me on that day, 'Lord, Lord, did we not prophesy in your name, and in your name drive out demons and perform many miracles?' Then I will tell them plainly, 'I never knew you. Away from me, you evildoers!'"

We may fool the preacher. We may fool family members. We may even be able to fool ourselves into thinking that we are genuine believers, but we can't fool God. The Scriptures declare, "Nothing in all creation is hidden from God's sight. Everything is uncovered and laid bare before the eyes of him to whom we must give account" (Hebrews 4:13).

However, there is tremendous news in that if we put our trust in Jesus Christ and what He did at Calvary, we can be converted. Yes, God is even able to transform an undesirable fish into "a keeper"! "Therefore, if anyone is in Christ, he is a new creation; the old has gone, the new has come!" (2 Corinthians 5:17) When the Lord returns, what kind of fish will you be? Allow Him to make you "a keeper." Better yet, a real trophy!

Prayer: *Heavenly Father, help me live my life in such a way that others know You are real. I ask this in Jesus' name. Amen.*

POWDER AND PULL
Scripture Reading: James 5:13-18

Do your prayers reach heaven?

When I first started shooting my old recurve, I developed the nasty habit of not taking a full draw. I would pull the bow all the way back, but then relax the string just before release. As a result my arrow often dropped short of its mark.

Then, somewhere I read that it was helpful to gradually increase the draw just before releasing as a way of compensating. This has helped, but there are still times when I slip back into my old habit.

It's sad to say, but sometimes our prayers are like arrows from partially drawn bows or powderless bullets. In order for them to reach their destination, they should have some powder and pull behind them.

In today's text we see that Elijah's prayers were neither half-hearted nor haphazard. He prayed specifically and with great determination. James informs us, "He prayed earnestly that it would not rain" (James 5:17). God yearns for our prayers to be like Elijah's. God doesn't want us to mechanically go through some ritual. Our prayers can, and should be, hot with desire and filled with faith.

Prayer: *Heavenly Father, forgive me for the times when I merely go through a ritual instead of crying out to You with all my heart. Thank You for Jesus who makes it possible to boldly approach the throne of grace. Amen.*

DOING WHAT GOD DESIGNED
Scripture Reading: Ephesians 2:6-10

We have a female English pointer who is a joy to watch in the field. She is primarily white with black spots and ticking, has a short sleek coat, and carries herself elegantly. We call her "Cookie" but her actual registered name is "Divine Arrow."

To see her on point is a powerful experience. One can't help but think about the centuries of selective breeding that took place—as well as the invisible God who ultimately stands behind such ability. A while back I found myself patting her on the side saying, "Girl, you were made to do this!"

Periodically we all find ourselves in a job (or doing something as part of our job) that seems less than significant. Sometimes God may be calling us to switch careers or it may be He simply expects us to persevere.

I've come to the conclusion that what makes a job truly significant is not so much what we are doing, but rather why and for whom we are performing the task. Jesus said that even such a common thing as a cup of water can wind up being worthy of a reward. He told His disciples, "I tell you the truth, anyone who gives you a cup of water in my name because you belong to Christ will certainly not lose his reward" (Mark 9:41). Later, Paul reminded the Christians in Corinth that God could be honored by the ordinary activity of eating and drinking. He said, "So whether you eat or drink or whatever you do, do it all for the glory of God" (1 Corinthians 10:31). How about you? Are you doing what you were created to do? Are you doing it for the glory of God?

Prayer: *Heavenly Father, help me to be and do all that I can for Your glory. In Jesus' name. Amen.*

GOD NEVER MISSES
Scripture Reading: Hebrews 2:1-4

His thick beams, long tines, and heavy body made him the type of buck about which every deer hunter dreams. Yet, this was no dream. This was the real thing! The big bruiser accompanied by a couple of does was in an open field and headed straight toward me.

When the huge twelve-pointer turned broadside, I squeezed the trigger—BOOM! The slug zipped past. "How could I have missed?" Struggling to maintain my composure, I quickly levered in the next round. Then, just as the whitetail started to quarter away—BOOM! I missed again, and then again!

The truth is I've missed a lot of times in my life. Not only have I missed with rifles, shotguns, and bows, I have also missed morally. I deserve hell. I deserve the arrow of God's wrath. And that's a scary thought because God never misses. That's right, never!

In the Bible we are told about a bow that was drawn by no one special—and it's arrow released without a precise target in mind. Nevertheless, this particular arrow hit the bull's-eye. The Word of God states, "But someone drew his bow at random and hit the king of Israel between the sections of his armor" (1 Kings 22:34a). God was behind this bow. As a result, in one swift flight of an arrow, the wicked rule of powerful King Ahab came to an abrupt halt. And it happened even though Ahab had tried to disguise himself in battle. Furthermore, the fulfillment of a prophecy of God's judgment made by a man named Micaiah (1 Kings 22:28) and another pronouncement made by Elijah (1 Kings 21:19) was also set in motion.

You see, it seemed that Ahab had gotten away with many terrible things. We are told in the Scriptures concerning him that, "There was never a man like Ahab, who sold himself to do evil in the eyes of the Lord, urged on by Jezebel his wife" (1 Kings 21:25). However, judgment finally fell on this evildoer. Ahab, despite his protective armor and a clever disguise, could not escape God's judgment.

The fact is, apart from a personal relationship with Jesus Christ, no one can escape the wrath of God. As the writer of Hebrews asked, "How shall we escape if we ignore such a great salvation?" (Hebrews 2:3) But the Good News is that Christ has paid the price for our sin. Indeed, "Since we have now been justified by his blood, how much more shall we be saved from God's wrath through him!" (Romans 5:9). With Christ there is no need for worry.

Prayer: *Heavenly Father, thank You for sending Your Son "Jesus, who rescues us from the coming wrath" (1 Thessalonians 1:10b). Help me to remember the great price that was paid. In Jesus' name. Amen.*

THE SNAKE
Scripture Reading: Joshua 1:6-9

The snake was curled up next to a rock just five feet away from the place where I was fly fishing. Although I had managed to take a rainbow trout with a fly a few minutes earlier, having now seen a snake laying by a rock along this South Dakota stream certainly cramped my style. Of course, the sign posted at the trailhead, which warned of rattle snakes, didn't help much either!

You see, I have a personal list of certain creatures in this world that make me uncomfortable. Snakes happen to be on that list and are only slightly outranked by rats and bats. Nevertheless, I kept on fishing, but started relegating more and more space to this reptile by the rock.

Early the next morning, I hiked back to the same spot, but again found myself avoiding the rock where I had seen the snake the day before. Although the snake was now nowhere to be seen, I still skirted around the area where the serpent had been as if it were now sacred snake ground or was surrounded by some sort of invisible fence.

I started thinking, "Why should this serpent (which was no longer visible) be able to control my footsteps?" And again, "If, I come back to fish in the same place ten years from now, will I still be afraid of the snake by the rock?" Suddenly I found myself purposely and victoriously (with one eye looking for the snake!) fly fishing right next to the rock!

Fear has a way of fencing off certain areas of our life. In what ways have fears or painful experiences of the past prevented you from going where you wanted to go, doing what you wanted to do, or being who you wanted to be? Perhaps the painful memory of a broken relationship prevents you from reaching out to another. Or, maybe a previous failure in a business venture has paralyzed your ability to step out and take a risk.

The fact is, we are either controlled by our fears or we control them. When preparing to enter the promised land the Lord told Joshua, "Be strong and courageous. Do not be terrified; do not be discouraged, for the Lord your God will be with you wherever you go" (Joshua 1:9). God didn't want Joshua to be controlled by fear, nor does He want that for us. Friend, let's not allow fear to control us, but instead let's choose to tread on our fears by trusting in the living God. Like King David we can say, "When I am afraid, I will trust in you" (Psalm 56:3).

Prayer: *Heavenly Father, may You help me to always master fear. Fill me with faith and courage. I ask this in the name of Jesus. Amen.*

ALL SHAKEN UP!
Scripture Reading: 2 Thessalonians 1:1-10

The buck came busting out of a patch of brush and headed straight toward my tree stand. Within seconds he had crossed a field and was ready to jump a fence less than five feet from the base of my tree. At first glimpse of this wide-racked whitetail, my iron sights were drawn to his chest. However, I opted for the easy broadside shot he was bound to present. He approached the sagging section of barbed wire. Then, just as I started to squeeze off that one sure shot—CLUNK! The side of my rifle hit a limb. I panicked and fired a poor shot anyway—it clearly missed. He bounded over the fence as I awkwardly managed to get my rifle to the other side of the large limb. However, the lower branches on the opposite side of the tree forced me to wait for a clear shot. By the time the buck came into the open, I was all shaken up! Frantically, I fired three more rounds as he disappeared around the hill. I never saw him again.

I had done my preseason scouting, prepared a stand, and picked out at least a dozen shooting lanes. Although I had mentally planned for about every possible scenario with which I might be presented, I wasn't ready. The Bible tells us that most people won't be ready when Jesus Christ returns. It's not that individuals won't have plans. However, their plans will be short-sighted. They will be concerned about the things of this life and not with the life to come. Jesus once said about His return, "Just as it was in the days of Noah, so also will it be in the days of the Son of Man. People were eating, drinking, marrying and being given in marriage up to the day Noah entered the ark. Then the flood came and destroyed them all" (Luke 17:26-27).

It's sad, but many hunters will devote much time thinking about where to hunt this fall, but little about where they will wind up spending eternity. However, God wants each one of us to be ready. The prophet Amos told the people of his day, "Prepare to meet your God" (4:12).

Prayer: Lord Jesus, may You bring people to know You before it's too late. Thank You for the gift of eternal life and the opportunity to know the only true God. In Your name. Amen.

THE ANCIENT TRADITION OF HUNTING
Scripture Reading: Genesis 9:1-7

How long has hunting been around? It obviously predates compounds, fiberglass recurves, and aluminum arrows. We all realize that hunting existed long before the invention of double odd buck and black powder rifles. Hunting even predates the U.S. Constitution, the pilgrims, and Native Americans who were here long before the Mayflower arrived.

The fact is, to learn about the early history of hunting a person needs to examine God's word, the Bible. According to the Scriptures, more than four thousand years ago a man named Nimrod was the first to become famous for his activities in the field. Sometime after the flood in Noah's day (Genesis 6-9) and before the confusion of language at Babel (Genesis 11:1-9), Nimrod appeared on the stage of human history. The Bible says concerning him, "He was a mighty hunter before the Lord; that is why it is said, 'Like Nimrod, a mighty hunter before the Lord'" (Genesis 10:9).

Nevertheless, to arrive at the very fountain head of hunting, we must ultimately turn to God. It was He who told Noah, "Everything that lives and moves will be food for you. Just as I gave you the green plants, I now give you everything" (Genesis 9:3). Later, in Leviticus 17:13-14, the Lord gave the Israelites some specific hunting regulations.

Prayer: *Lord God, may I obey game regulations in such a way that my life reflects a relationship with You. I ask this in Jesus' name. Amen.*

RABBIT HUNT ROMANCE
Scripture Reading: Genesis 2:18-25

It was a Wisconsin winter's day that was about to turn nasty. Nevertheless, I will always remember that pivotal snowy Saturday back in January of 1988.

You see, I was a bachelor—a single pastor of a small country church. I knew that there were people in the church praying for me to find a mate. I think they felt sorry for me—and (unless something radical happened) they considered me doomed to an unhealthy lifetime diet that mostly consisted of frozen chicken and french fries. As a matter of fact, the blackened cookie sheets and warped pizza pan tins stuck in the snow outside the back of the church parsonage were visible proof of my poor eating habits—as well as a deep disdain for doing dishes.

At the age of thirty-one, family and friends had finally quit asking if I was ever going to get married. They evidently figured I had settled on a life of perpetual bachelorhood. Furthermore, the odds of my taking a young lady rabbit hunting on a first date and having it develop into something serious was certainly a longshot.

Now I have to admit that Beth was not the first female that had accompanied me on a hunt. There were others that had tagged along on deer hunts or raccoon hunts. But this was my first time hunting cottontails in which I was accompanied by a young woman.

Beth was a city girl who had never even held a gun—let alone whack a rabbit. But, after picking her up and then informing her what we would be doing—she was still game to go hunting.

We traveled to a wooded farm owned by my parents. After a brief time of target practice, we made our way up the hill through the knee high snow toward a patch of berry briars.

We hadn't gone far when a rabbit raced up the hill—and stopped. Beth pulled up the twenty-gauge single-shot Beretta—and squeezed the trigger. Boom! The recoil from the shotgun caused her to land backward in the snow. In fact, I'm pretty sure that Beth hit the ground before the rabbit did. She was still laughing as I pulled her to her feet. I raced up the hill to retrieve the cottontail.

Beth was carrying a twenty-gauge shotgun, and I a .22 caliber pistol. However, Cupid must have been packing a double barrel twelve-gauge that day because I started to get smitten. About eleven months later we were married—and today we have four wonderful daughters.

But the fact is, ours was not the first romance ignited in an outdoor setting. For example, Adam and Eve were united in a beautiful garden by God Himself. One could accurately call this the first garden wedding (Genesis 2).

Later the book of Genesis chapter twenty-four relates how Rebekah (who eventually became Isaac's wife) was discovered on the outskirts of a town working at a well. The Lord used thirsty camels and Rebekah's willingness to water them as a supernatural sign. By Rebekah's service she was clearly identified as the one who should become Isaac's wife.

It was also at a well of water that Moses and Zipporah initially met (Exodus 2). Moses was fleeing from Pharaoh. Although the outward circumstances were less than favorable, God was still in control. He caused Moses to meet his mate in an outdoor setting.

During the days when the judges ruled, a widow named Ruth from the country of Moab went out to glean grain. God was guiding and she happened to start gleaning in a field belonging to an older eligible bachelor named Boaz (Ruth 2). And, as they say, the rest is history.

The Lord is not limited in how He can bring people together. God can arrange romances in remote areas, and even on a rabbit hunt if He so desires!

Prayer: Lord God, thank You for Your guidance in every location and in every area of life—including marriage. Amen.

GOD IN THE ORDINARY
Scripture Reading: Matthew 17:24-27

Have you ever caught a fish with a coin in its mouth? You probably know a lot of people who fish—but how many could honestly answer "yes"?

However, I remember hearing about a fellow who caught some dentures while deep sea fishing. The false teeth were found in the belly of a fish he happened to land. Eventually these human choppers were reunited with the gums of their rightful owner—an owner who had accidentally lost them overboard a number of months earlier.

Now admittedly this is a pretty amazing story. Especially when one contemplates the odds of having their teeth return from the depths. Indeed, the depths of an enormously vast sea!

Even so, in the Bible we have a record regarding an event even more remarkable. It's a true angling account which not only shows the supernatural power of Christ—but also reveals His unlimited ability to use ordinary things to provide in an unusual way.

In Matthew chapter seventeen, Peter was asked whether or not Christ paid the temple tax. But, before Peter could even question Jesus about this matter—Christ asked him a couple of thought-provoking questions. Jesus opted to pay the tax and then went on to tell Peter, "But so that we may not offend them, go to the lake and throw out your line. Take the first fish you catch; open its mouth and you will find a four-drachma coin. Take it and give it to them for my tax and yours" (v. 27).

Now, I want to ask you, "What do you think the probability was of Peter catching just such a fish?" Remember he was to accomplish this with a simple hook rather than a wide net. And, that Peter would actually be the fortunate fisherman (rather than someone else) to catch this swimming piggy bank is even more mind-boggling.

But, in addition to all this, the chances of Peter finding a coin of specific value in the mouth (not the stomach) of the very first fish he pulled up (not the second, third, or fourth that he caught)—must also be entered into the equation. Why the chances are so slim—it's almost enough to make the Lottery look like a sure thing!

Indeed the Lord of the universe sometimes uses common things in unordinary ways. In fact, God can use anything. Down through Bible history God has used things like: a bush that didn't burn, a staff that turned into a snake, a donkey that was made to talk, ravens that brought food to a prophet, etc. In this instance the Lord used a line, a hook, a fish, a lake, and a certain sized coin. A coin that must have smelled a little fishy when Peter went to pay the tax!

While it is true that often "God is found in the details", we can also find Him in the plain and ordinary things of life. Let's look for Him!

Prayer: *Lord God, thank You for being able to use even the ordinary things of life. May You use me in a supernatural way for Your glory. I ask this in Jesus' name. Amen.*

SIGN
Scripture Reading: Psalm 8

The most successful deer hunters that I know have learned the importance of looking for sign. The fact is, even an elusive whitetail buck can't help but leave evidence of his presence behind. There may be a long, heavy track, an oversize bed, or even a highly visible rub on a thigh-sized tree. But in any case, a buck always leaves his mark. It's true that we may never see the rack that peeled back the bark, the huge body that made the bed, or the hoof that left the track. But, then again, there's a chance that we will.

The Creator of the universe who made all things has also left His mark. In fact, the Apostle Paul pointed out that the signs of God's presence are so numerous that everyone knows something about Him. As a result, no one has a valid reason for not acknowledging His existence. Paul pointed out to the Christians in Rome, "For since the creation of the world God's invisible qualities—his eternal power and divine nature—have been clearly seen, being understood from what has been made, so that men are without excuse" (Romans 1:20). Yes, God has left the prints of His invisible fingers all over creation. All that He has made carries a label that identifies Him as the Maker.

Prayer: *Heavenly Father, thank You for Your many signatures, but thank You most of all for Your Son, Jesus Christ who said, "Anyone who has seen me has seen the Father" (John 14:9). Amen.*

THE BIBLE AND MODERN HUNTING WEAPONS
Scripture Reading: Leviticus 17:13-14

What does the Bible say about modern hunting methods? At the present time there continues to be different views even among members of the hunting community as to what type of weapon is acceptable for hunting. Heated discussions over the use of the compound bow verses the recurve or longbow is one such example.

However, it is important to note that the Bible does not focus upon the appropriateness of hunting as it pertains to the weapon or method used. Rather, there is an emphasis upon the types of game which can be taken (Deuteronomy 14:5) and the manner in which blood of the animal or birds harvested are to be handled (Leviticus 17:13-14). In the Bible, blood represents the life of a creature. Therefore, the way a person would adhere to this regulation in the book of Leviticus regarding blood very clearly revealed the importance of having a reverence for life.

In the wisdom literature, we even find that the person who harvests game and does not take care of what he has harvested received the admonition, "The lazy man does not roast his game, but the diligent man prizes his possessions" (Proverbs 12:27). Nevertheless, in the Bible we have no clear guidelines that pertain to hunting instruments.

Prayer: Father, thank You for being involved in the hunting realm. You are truly the God of every generation and all of creation. May all that I do bring glory to You! I ask this in Jesus' name. Amen.

WHO OWNS THE LAND?
Scripture Reading: Psalm 24:1-2

Sadly, many people who have never spent much time in the Scriptures have tried to blame Christianity or the teachings of the Bible for certain environmental problems. They do this even though an honest glance at other countries in which the predominate religious culture could accurately be classified as atheistic, Buddhist, Hinduistic, or Islamic have lands which have been ravaged. Even the late well-known and greatly revered conservationist Aldo Leopold got it wrong in this regard. In 1948 Saint Leopold (I say "saint" in that some admire him so highly) wrote in *A Sand County Almanac*, "Conservation is getting nowhere because it is incompatible with our Abrahamic concept of land. We abuse land because we regard it as a commodity belonging to us." He was certainly right in that land has often been viewed as a commodity that could be misused or abused. Nevertheless, Leopold was wrong if he really thought the roots of such destructive thinking can be traced back to the Bible.

On the contrary, when the Lord gave the land to the Hebrews, as He had promised the patriarch Abraham centuries before, it was always with the view that it actually belonged to God. While it is certainly true that specific portions of the promised land were to remain in each designated Israelite family and clan, this was always with the understanding that God retained ultimate ownership. He stated, "The land must not be sold permanently, because the land is mine and you are but aliens and my tenants" (Leviticus 25:23).

Again, we further learn that it is not just some large lot in the ancient Near East that the Lord of the universe possesses. The fact is, the Lord owns everything. He told Moses on Mount Sinai, "Now if you obey me fully and keep my covenant, then out of all nations you will be my treasured possession. Although the whole earth is mine" (Exodus 19:5).

In addition, not just the land, but everything on it (including all wildlife) belongs to God. In Psalm fifty the Lord made it known to His people that He did not need their cattle for a sacrifice. He said, "I have no need of a bull from your stall or of goats from your pens" (9). He then went on to explain why: "For every animal of the forest is mine, and the cattle on a thousand hills. I know every bird in the mountains, and the creatures of the field are mine. If I were hungry I would not tell you, for the world is mine, and all that is in it" (Psalm 50:11-12). According to the Bible no nation, ethnic group, state, county, township, conservation group, radical environmental group, DNR bureaucratic branch, or individual can really lay a lasting claim to a piece of property and the wildlife that resides thereon. After all, "The earth is the Lord's, and everything in it" (Psalm 24:1a). The Bible teaches that we are all temporary stewards and managers who will one day have to give an account to the Eternal Landlord.

Prayer: Lord, keep me mindful of the fact that everything belongs to You. Not only do You own the cattle on a thousand hills, but You also own the hills. May I be faithful with all that You entrust me—for Christ's sake. Amen.

OLD FISHERMEN NEVER . . . .
Scripture Reading: Hebrews 9:27-28

I was fishing a tributary on the north shore of Lake Superior. Below the spot where I was standing, the powerful swirling river cut its way between high rock cliffs, around big boulders, and then poured into the brilliant blue Great Lake. Just above me water continually rumbled, tumbled, and thundered through a rugged, rocky gorge. The sights and sounds were absolutely spectacular!

I don't know about you, but it is at times like this, and in places like this, that my deepest thoughts seem to surface. For example, I often think about the brevity of my life. I marvel at how a river I'm fishing has been running night and day, century after century, long before I was born, and that it will (unless the Lord returns first and shuts it off) be running day and night long after I leave this planet. As the Old Testament preacher observed, "All streams flow into the sea, yet the sea is never full. To the place the streams come from, there they return again" (Ecclesiastes 1:7).

However, on this particular occasion I contemplated the profound role fishing had played in my life and in the life of our entire family. For instance, there was my grandfather whom I never met. Although my grandfather might have felt the river's rumbling, he couldn't have heard its loud sounds. You see, he became totally deaf at age three.

Even so, Grandpa was a fisherman. In fact, he died with a fishing pole in his hand! My dad (who was twenty-one at the time) found him after he had failed to return from a time of fishing. Grandpa's tracks indicated that he died in mid-stride. As he went to take a next step—he fell backward. There his body lay between the river and his earthly home along with a number of fish he had caught and the rod he was carrying.

Later, I got to thinking about my older brother, Mick. Like my grandfather, as well as my dad, he had a real passion for fishing. The day after his twentieth birthday he and his best friend went to the Mississippi river in order to fish. On their return that evening, there was a wreck. Mick was killed instantly when the car in which he was riding accidentally struck the back of a semi. My brother died in his sleep—not with a rod in his hand, but with one in the car.

Many of us have seen plaques or read postcards inscribed with the words, "Old fishermen never die, they just smell that way!" Now, while it's true that active anglers can and often do carry a strange fishy aroma, they are not immune from death. Indeed, old and young anglers alike can be yanked out of this life. As the writer of Ecclesiastes explained, "No man knows when his hour will come: As fish are caught in a cruel net, or birds are taken in a snare, so men are trapped by evil times that fall unexpectedly upon them" (9:12).

Friend, are you prepared to leave this world? Have you received Jesus Christ as your Lord and Savior? If not, don't delay! Because, like my grandfather who died in mid-step or brother Mick who left this world in his sleep, so we "do not know what a day may bring forth" (Proverbs 27:1b).

Prayer: *Heavenly Father, thank You for sending Your Son, Jesus, in order that I might live forever. Help me to live each day as if it might be my last. In Christ's name. Amen.*

THE GREAT DIVIDE
Scripture Reading: Ephesians 5:25-32

In recent years, there has been a growing chasm between some hunters and non-hunters. This division is not physical, but rather philosophical or theological in nature. And, whether we want to admit it or not, this gap doesn't seem to be narrowing. Furthermore, some of the inappropriate arguments that individuals from both sides have used to support their cause have clouded the real issues.

Take, for example, the positive financial factors that some draw on to defend hunting. Even though economic matters may be important, this type of reasoning never addresses the moral issue about which many non-hunters are asking. We also need to remember that just because an activity may prove to be financially beneficial to a few, or even to many, does not necessarily justify that particular activity (see 1 Timothy 6:10). Certainly there were some in this country who, in the past century, profited from human slavery. However, this never made slavery right.

With the same token, others have tried to take truths from the Bible in order to prove that hunting is wrong. The command, "Thou shalt not kill," (Exodus 20:13, KJV) has been used by some to say that God clearly condemns the taking of any creature's life. Nevertheless, to do so one must seriously distort the intended meaning of this Scripture and also remove the passage from its original context.

First of all, the Hebrew term which is translated "kill" by the King James Version addresses the taking of another person's life or what we commonly call "murder." The context of this particular Bible verse also makes this clear. And if Exodus 20:13 was intended for animals, why did God direct the Israelites to sacrifice sheep, goats, and cattle (Exodus 20:24), to stone a bull that gores someone to death (Exodus 21:28), and use certain types of skins in constructing the tabernacle (Exodus 26:14)?

On the contrary, the Bible reveals that we have a responsibility before God to speak what is right. This even applies to issues that pertain to hunting.

Prayer: *Heavenly Father, help me to see things from Your perspective. May I recognize truth by what Your word says. I ask this in Jesus' name. Amen.*

Devotions for Hunters & Anglers

OLD ANTLERS NEVER DIE . . . BUT THEY WILL BURN!
Scripture Reading: 2 Peter 3:1-14

A while back a friend of mine had a fire in his garage. Not only did Louis lose his building and the normal contents one would expect to find there, but he also lost his compound bow, portable tree stand, and (perhaps even tougher to take!) more than two dozen whitetail racks that were hung inside. Later, when he and family members sifted through the debris, they managed to find only a small chunk of one antler. Everything else had gone up in flames.

I have to say that this individual took it quite well. Better than I'm sure I ever would. Louis somehow managed to keep these material things, and even those with sentimental value, in their proper perspective.

Nevertheless, when you stop to think about it, every single antler will one day be turned into ashes. According to the Scriptures, there is coming a time when the entire physical world as we know it will be burned up. This will come about when Jesus Christ returns to judge the earth. The Bible tells us, "The heavens will disappear with a roar; the elements will be destroyed by fire, and the earth and everything in it will be laid bare" (2 Peter 3:10b). Yes, there is coming a time when all the physical things that we hold dear in this world will be dissolved.

Indeed, we need to realize that the material things of this world, which we so frequently allow to capture our affection and hard-earned currency, are fading away. That's right. Every rifle, bow, boat, cabin, car, and truck will eventually be dissolved. This fact should have a powerful effect upon encouraging us to live in a manner which is pleasing to God. As Peter challenged his readers, "Since everything will be destroyed in this way, what kind of people ought you to be?" (2 Peter

3:11a).

Prayer: Lord Jesus, help me to live for what is eternal. Amen.

SINCERITY ISN'T ENOUGH
Scripture Reading: Titus 3:3-8

Sometimes being sincere just isn't enough. The fact is, even where we choose to wet our line can make a world of difference. We can try and fish in a big, beautiful swimming pool or in a tiny mud puddle, but if there are no fish in either, we will be disappointed. We can try every lure or live bait imaginable. We can even look sincere—but sincerity isn't enough.

Many people have said, "It doesn't matter what a person believes, just as long as they're sincere." But this is simply not true. Some sincere people have blown themselves up or hijacked airplanes and flown them into tall buildings thinking such an act would help get them into heaven. Still others are convinced that if they do enough good deeds or if they try to keep the Ten Commandments, it will make them right with God. But again, sincerity just isn't enough!

Indeed, it is not in what we can do for God, "not by works, so that no one can boast" (Ephesians 2:9), nor by keeping the Mosaic Law, "because by observing the law no one will be justified" (Galatians 2:16). Rather, being right with God involves accepting what God has done for us.

You see, sincerity isn't enough, but Jesus Christ's sacrifice for our sins on the cross is! Trust Him!

Prayer: *Lord God, thank You for paying the price for all my sin. Thank You for Your wonderful grace. Help me to be a sincere follower of You all the days of my life. I ask this in Jesus' name. Amen.*

THE VISION
Scripture Reading: Exodus 20:1-17

    Even after asking Jesus Christ to forgive me of my sins, the peace I was longing for continued to elude me. I especially remember one night when I was experiencing an intense inner struggle. I knew that there was something that was not right between God and me, but I failed to figure out what it was. I wept and cried out to the Lord yet found no peace.

    Then, for no apparent reason, I stopped praying, and pulled back a window curtain by the bed where I was kneeling. I looked outside and watched as a cloud passed in front of the bright, silvery, full moon. There, in the cloud in a moment's time, I saw the perfect silhouette of a deer, a fish, and a hand. The hand was cupped and turned up as though holding something. I saw all three of these silhouettes simultaneously—and yet they appeared in a consecutive order. Words fail to adequately describe the vision.

    At the time, I could not understand what it meant. I knew that deer hunting and trout fishing were an extremely important part of my life. Nevertheless, it didn't dawn on me that this might be the reason I was experiencing such turmoil.

    The next morning I drove straight to the small secular junior college where I had started taking classes. The dean of the college was a Christian and had previously shared with me some of the miraculous things that God had done in her life. I hoped she would be able to tell me the meaning of what I had seen. I didn't even know how to describe this experience. I thought this might be what could be called a "vision."

    I no more stepped into her office before I blurted out what I had seen. She simply responded, "Well, the Bible says, 'Thou shalt have no other gods before me.'" As she quoted these words from Exodus 20:3 (KJV) I immediately knew that this was what God had been trying to convey to me. She then went on to say, "God isn't telling you that you can not hunt and fish, but these things must not be more important to you than He is. God has to be in first place." She then explained that the cupped hand signified, "You are in God's hand."

That experience took place in 1978, but I remember it as if it happened yesterday. However, we don't have to have a vision to know these truths. All we have to do is read God's word, the Bible.

Not only does the Bible make it clear that God deserves and desires to have first place in our lives. The Scriptures also tell us that if we know Jesus Christ as our personal Lord and Savior we are held securely in His hand. In John chapter ten, Jesus said, "My sheep listen to my voice; I know them, and they follow me. I give them eternal life, and they shall never perish; no one can snatch them out of my hand. My Father, who gave them to me, is greater than all; no one can snatch them out of my Father's hand" (vv. 27-29).

Prayer: *Father, help me to seek You and Your kingdom above all else. In Jesus' name. Amen.*

DIVINE DIVIDEND
Scripture Reading: Matthew 19:16-30

The large buck's rack glistened in the morning sun as he crossed the open valley behind the barn. It was a beautiful sight and I wept as I watched.

But tears weren't running down my cheeks because I had been touched by nature's grandeur. No, the reason I was weeping had to do with surrendering a part of my life to Jesus Christ—an area that I still sometimes struggle keeping under control.

The sight that morning out the back barn door where I was milking cows made it seem like God was rubbing salt in my wound. You see, a few weeks before the season I became convinced that God wanted me to give up deer hunting. However, that was one thing I did not want to do. It became even more difficult when the farmer I was working for that year offered to post his entire farm. Besides the cropland, this farmer had over three hundred acres of standing timber. It was, and still is, some of the best deer country in central Wisconsin. And, I could have hunted it all without having to compete with other hunters.

But now, as the buck made his way across the stubbled corn field my mind was filled with doubts. I could no longer buy a license—it was too late. The rifle season had already opened.

At first I was mad at God. I thought, "How could you ask me to give up something I enjoy so much?" Then later, I started wondering if maybe I had gone crazy. Or, perhaps I had merely fooled myself into believing that this was what God wanted me to do. Or worse yet, what if the devil was trying to use me to turn others away from Christ? After all, what dedicated deer hunter would be drawn to Christ by my giving up hunting?

Well, to make a long story short, I managed to

make it through that deer season and decided not to hunt the next one either. God taught me a great deal during those two years about things like pride, greed, and selfishness. I began to see how prevalent it was in my life and other hunters as well. As a matter of fact, the Lord is still cleaning a whole lot of these wrong motives and desires out of my life.

Nevertheless, when the third year finally rolled around, I knew that the Lord wanted me to hunt. And, needless to say, He didn't have to twist my arm too hard to talk me into it! That year I ended up harvesting the biggest buck that I have taken up to the present time. Now he was no record breaker. For some I suppose he could have been merely classified as "a nice buck" or "a dandy."

But the point is this. I am convinced it was not by coincidence that this buck was harvested after I surrendered this area of my life to Christ. Nor was it by accident that a fellow hunter who knew my situation and whom I had been trying to win to the Lord remarked out of the blue, "Tom, you gave your deer hunting to God and He allowed you to get that big buck!"

No, these things didn't take place by chance. I believe God wanted me and others who hunted with me to know that He is intimately involved in every aspect of life. And, when we give something to God He either replaces it with something better or makes up for it in another way.

Now more than likely the Lord is not going to ask you to give up deer hunting. However, He might want you to make some major modifications in the way or with whom you hunt.

Surrendering your deer hunting to Christ won't guarantee that you will tag a bigger buck this season. But it will make you grateful in the long run. Jesus told His disciples that those who give up things for His sake will eventually "receive a hundred times as much" (Matthew 19:29). It is important to keep in mind that the Lord of the universe pays divine dividends!

Prayer: Heavenly Father, thank You for keeping track of our tiny sacrifices. Help me to trust You even when I don't understand. I ask this in Jesus' name. Amen.

THE UNSEEN BATTLE
Scripture Reading: Ephesians 6:10-20

Each and every fall whitetail bucks begin bashing their antlers together. Have you ever had the privilege of witnessing two whitetail deer battling it out? These sometimes ferocious fights take place each and every fall during what is commonly called "the rut." Still, very few of these fights (even though perhaps millions of them take place on an annual basis) are ever seen by any human eye.

On the other hand, the faithful Christian is involved in a year-round spiritual rumble. Furthermore, our supernatural struggle is not merely against other human beings. On the contrary, as the Apostle Paul pointed out, "Our struggle is not against flesh and blood, but against the rulers, against the authorities, against the powers of this dark world and against the spiritual forces of evil in the heavenly realms" (Ephesians 6:12). Whether we are aware of it or not, there is an intense spiritual contest taking place all around us. Indeed, there is a war being waged between wickedness and righteousness every minute of every day.

How about you? Are you faithfully fighting against the powers of darkness—or are you waging battle for them? You see, if we are not completely committed to Jesus Christ, we are against Him. Christ made it clear that we can't straddle the fence. We can not simply stand on middle ground. Jesus Himself said, "He who is not with me is against me, and he who does not gather with me scatters" (Matthew 12:30). Friend, are you gathering or scattering?

Prayer: *Our Heavenly Father, thank You for giving us the weapons and the will to be able to stand against the powers of darkness. Help me to stand firm. I ask this in the name of Jesus. Amen.*

FAITH: AN ESSENTIAL INGREDIENT
Scripture Reading: Galatians 3:1-14

Every whitetail hunter exercises faith. In fact, when you stop to think about it, deer hunting requires an enormous amount of faith. This is true regardless of whether one hunts with a bow or a rifle.

The bowhunter trusts in the stand being used, string or cable pulled, and broadheads attached. The person using bow and arrow must also place a measure of faith in one's own ability to accurately judge distance and the anatomy of a deer.

Faith is a requirement for the rifle hunter as well. To hunt with a rifle requires faith in the firearm carried, the company producing the ammunition, and the area being hunted.

Yes, from the onset, when we first purchase our hunting license (which fails to come with a money-back guarantee!) until we kneel down to fasten the site tag—we use faith.

Salvation also requires faith. However, instead of placing our trust in a number of things, we put our trust entirely in one person—the Lord Jesus Christ. Our faith rests in what Jesus Christ has done for us on the cross, not in what we have done or can do for Him. If we could be made right with God by going through some ritual or performing some good deed, Christ would never have needed to come and die on the cross. As Paul reminded the Galatians, "If righteousness could be gained through the law, Christ died for nothing!" (Galatians 2:21)

Prayer: *Father, thank You for sending Your Son. Forgive me for the times when I place more faith in things and people than I do in You. Help me to be a person filled with faith in You. In the name of Jesus. Amen.*

IT WAS A DARK AND STORMY NIGHT
Scripture Reading: Psalm 56:3-4

It was a dark and stormy night (it really was!) and I was raccoon hunting alone on the backside of our Wisconsin dairy farm. The dogs ran a raccoon out of a corn strip and took it around the hill. Queenie and Penny (two of our blueticks) were soon treeing hard a couple hundred yards away on top the neighbor's ridge.

However, I just couldn't make my seventeen-year-old legs make that trek to the tree. There was nothing hindering me physically. All I had to do was cross one rusty barbed-wire fence, go through an old cemetery. . . . But wait, that was the problem. There was something inside of me that just would not let me cross that fence and step into the graveyard. It was an old, tiny place of internment and I was familiar with the headstones that marked the hand full of people buried there. In fact, during the daylight hours I had crossed through the middle of that cemetery many times. Nevertheless, doing it on a dark and stormy night just seemed too spooky! Indeed, fear had taken over. So, instead of traveling some 200 yards to the tree, I walked about 500 yards back to the farm buildings.

After arriving back at the house, I eventually talked my girlfriend (who was visiting with my family while I hunted) into hopping in the car with me and retrieving the dogs from a road located on the other side of where they were treeing. I remember I said something like this to her, "Come on, you need to experience this!" But the truth of the matter was that I was afraid to go alone.

How about you? What are you afraid of? If we are willing to admit it, we all either have been, or presently are, afraid of something.

Multitudes are now terrified of terrorism, while still others fear such diverse things as: heights, bats, snakes, showing emotion, spiders, crowds, being left alone, open places, death, and even dirty restrooms. Some fears are healthy and help protect us from harm. The Bible says, "The fear of the Lord is a fountain of life" (Proverbs 14:27a). However, many fears are unhealthy and can either prevent or cripple us from living the kind of life God desires.

King David is often remembered as being a fearless fighter. He not only took on a bear, lion, and an experienced warrior named Goliath while still a youth (1 Samuel 17), but David's entire life was marked with dangerous battles. Was he ever afraid when facing these life and death situations? Sure he was! However, the Bible tells us that when King David experienced fear he chose to combat his fear with faith. David told the Lord, "When I am afraid, I will trust in you" (Psalm 56:3). The presence and power of God was his comfort. David said, "Even though I walk through the valley of the shadow of death, I will fear no evil, for you are with me" (Psalm 23:4). If we have God in our life—there is no need to be afraid. Like David, we too can choose to combat our fears (even a fear of death) with faith in the living God!

Prayer: *Lord God, help me to choose to trust You when fear starts to overwhelm me. Help me to live a life filled with faith and not a life controlled by fear. I ask this in Jesus' name. Amen.*

COUNTING THE COST
Scripture Reading: Luke 14:25-35

Many times whitetail hunting has been made to look easy. There are virtually hundreds of products which are advertised as the surefire way of getting your deer. These companies say that if you use their scent, call, tree stand, scope, bow, etc., you can't help but fill your tag.

Of course, many of these products are able to increase the odds of a successful hunt. However, their effectiveness is often greatly exaggerated. As a result, the overall picture of what is involved in harvesting a deer ends up being distorted. In reality, deer hunting frequently requires endless hours of sitting in the cold, climbing steep hills, or wading through wet marshes.

Unfortunately, a similar thing sometimes takes place when the gospel of Jesus Christ is presented. There are times when, in an attempt to make the message appealing, the messenger ends up watering down the message.

Now make no mistake about it, eternal life is absolutely free! The Bible tells us, "The gift of God is eternal life in Christ Jesus our Lord" (Romans 6:23). The Bible also makes it clear that our eternal salvation cannot be gained by our performing good works: "not by works, so that no one can boast" (Ephesians 2:9).

Even so, following Christ is still extremely difficult. But Jesus never diluted the price one must pay to be a follower. He was up-front about what it took. Jesus made it clear from the beginning that to be a disciple was indeed costly. He told the crowds of His day, "Any of you who does not give up everything he has cannot be my disciple" (Luke 14:33).

Prayer: *Lord, when I think the cost of following You seems too high—remind me of the price paid at Calvary.*

Thank You for making the cost of following You clear. May You find me faithful. I ask this in Jesus' name. Amen.

THE PRODIGAL POOCH
Scripture Reading: Luke 15:11-32

The neighbor pulled into the driveway and said excitedly, "Tom, I think I just found Black Jack!" I envisioned a partially decomposed body with a distinguishable bullet-hole in the hide.

You see, close to six weeks earlier during his exercise time, my dog, Black Jack, gambled on making a break for it and headed for the hills. Despite my frantic calling, he kept right on going.

During the next several weeks, I frequently drove around searching for Black Jack. On one occasion I heard him barking as he presumably pursued his prey along a heavily wooded, snow-covered ridge. I called him by name. The barking stopped for several minutes. But then, as if compelled by a force greater than himself, he continued on.

Eventually I figured the odds were against Black Jack returning alive and gave the remainder of his dog food to a friend to use. After all, it was highly probable someone had shot him for chasing deer or that he had died some other way. It wasn't that I was strongly attached to this particular hound. One of the reasons he had been given to me was because he was an older dog whose periodic choice to chase deer had made him virtually useless as a coon hound.

But now, sure enough, within a couple hundred yards of the country church where I was serving as pastor, we found him. My prodigal pooch had finally returned!

Nevertheless, his lifestyle over the previous month-and-a-half had reduced him to little more than a bunch of bones. That is, bones with skin stretched over them. In addition, his nose and ears were a mass of scabs and lacerations from running through briar patches.

Now, I want to ask you, what do you think I did to Black Jack when I found him? I'll tell you what I did. I ran into the house and grabbed the best that I had which consisted of half a ring of bologna and several dinner rolls. (Please note: watch your fingers when feeding a starving dog!) Although it took time, I was eventually able to nurse him back to health.

The fact is, whether we are willing to admit it or not, apart from a personal relationship with Jesus Christ, we are all like Black Jack. We all have run away. Indeed, the Scriptures reveal that, "We all, like sheep, have gone astray, each of us has turned to his own way" (Isaiah 53:6a). In Luke chapter fifteen, Jesus talks about a wayward son who squandered his inheritance. So we, when left to our own devices, waste our time and treasures.

The good news is we can return to the Lord and he will gladly receive us. In Luke fifteen, the father graciously welcomed his prodigal son when he finally came home. And no matter what you may have done or where you may be, God wants you to know that you can return. After all, Jesus has clearly promised, "whoever comes to me I will never drive away" (John 6:37).

Friend, return to your Maker and Master while there is still time. "For the wages of sin is death, but the gift of God is eternal life in Christ Jesus our Lord" (Romans 6:23). And that's no bologna!

Prayer: Father, thank You for Your willingness to receive all who return to You. Amen.

I STILL WISH!
Scripture Reading: Luke 12:35-48

It was barely daylight when I arrived at the brushy thicket that bordered our pasture. I was fifteen, and certainly had much to learn about deer hunting. Even so, I already knew that this little pocket I was entering often harbored a buck. My goal was to try and get a crack at him before those who were on stand had a chance.

Carefully and as quietly as possible, I bent over and stepped through the tight, but somewhat rusty, strands of barbed wire. I paused. There was no movement. There was no sound of rustling leaves. I thought, "Surely if this patch of woods held deer—they must have gone out way ahead of me."

I gave my pant leg a yank, and when I did the cloth ripped, the fence rattled—and CRASH! About twenty feet away my eyes caught a quick (but lasting) flash of a whitetail buck's heavy rack moving above the briars as he busted away through the undergrowth. Then, just like that, he was gone. And, although this transpired more than three decades ago—to this day I still wish I had been ready!

According to the Bible, when Christ returns to earth many people will be caught off guard. If He came today, would you be ready? Jesus warned His disciples, "You also must be ready, because the Son of Man will come at an hour when you do not expect him" (Luke 12:40).

Prayer: *Lord God, help me to always be ready for Your return! I ask this in Jesus' name. Amen.*

WAS JESUS A VEGETARIAN?
Scripture Reading: 1 Timothy 4:4-5

Some things are hard to swallow. Listening to animal rights activists attempting to transform Jesus Christ into a vegetarian is one of them! This type of misrepresentation should greatly disturb every Christian.

I am not against vegetarianism. However, I am opposed to people purposely misrepresenting the Scriptures and Christ Himself in order to promote their own agenda.

Sadly, some have tried to claim that Jesus was a vegetarian in order to build a case against hunting. This argument usually follows a simplistic line of reasoning and goes something like this: "Jesus was a vegetarian, therefore hunting is wrong." Or, "Hunting is wrong, therefore Jesus must have been a vegetarian."

Nevertheless, a search of the Scriptures reveals that the using of animals for food can ultimately be traced back to the Bible. Following the flood in Noah's day, God blessed Noah and his sons and then went on to tell them, "Everything that lives and moves will be food for you. Just as I gave you the green plants, I now give you everything" (Genesis 9:3). The Lord clearly permitted and even promoted the eating of animals.

Concerning Christ, we know that Jesus participated in the Passover meal as commanded in Exodus twelve. For the Hebrews, the Passover served as a significant reminder of an important time when the Lord delivered His people out of Egyptian bondage. The Passover celebration itself included (among other things) a meal with roast lamb. We know that the Lord Jesus ate the Passover. In fact, according to Luke twenty-two what we commonly call "The Last Supper" was actually the Passover. Therefore, Jesus Christ cannot be classified as a vegetarian.

We learn in the gospel of Mark that on one occasion

Jesus' disciples were criticized for not practicing a certain Jewish ceremonial washing. Christ responded to His critics by pointing out that it is not what goes into a person that makes an individual unclean, "Rather, it is what comes out of a man that makes him 'unclean'" (Mark 7:15). Jesus later went on to explain this statement to His followers by saying, "Don't you see that nothing that enters a man from the outside can make him 'unclean'? For it doesn't go into his heart but into his stomach, and then out of his body" (Mark 7:18-19a). In addition, a brief but revealing comment was made by the gospel writer when he wrote, "In saying this, Jesus declared all foods 'clean'" (Mark 7:19b). Jesus Christ did not cut meat out of the Jewish diet. By declaring "all foods clean" Christ actually expanded the menu of permissible foods which were previously listed in the Mosaic law!

According to the Scriptures, Jesus not only multiplied loaves and fishes in order to feed thousands, but after His resurrection we are told that the disciples "gave him a piece of broiled fish, and he took it and ate it in their presence" (Luke 24:42-43). By eating fish, the resurrected Christ cannot accurately be classified as a strict vegetarian.

The conclusion that Jesus was a vegetarian and therefore hunting is wrong has no foundation in Scripture. As a matter of fact, by looking at the Bible one finds that Jesus Christ was clearly not a vegetarian—nor did He ever advocate such a lifestyle. Jesus ate the Passover meal and also declared all foods clean. Furthermore, following His resurrection Christ consumed a piece of broiled fish in the presence of His disciples.

Prayer: *Father, protect society from the influence of all who seek to distort Your word. In Jesus' name. Amen.*

CATFISH CORNER
Scripture Reading: Romans 10:6-13

Not far from where I live there is a stop sign alongside a lake. It's a particular place which on spring nights has frequently been good for a nice cat fish or two—each at least a couple of feet long. It's also a place that has a soothing effect upon one's mind. Indeed, there is something special about sitting alone on that rocky bank after dark watching a calm moonlit lake. It is especially wonderful when such a relaxing night is then topped off with a tug on the line and a battle with a somewhat slow, but strong and deep-swimming catfish. In fact, there is seldom a time when I drive past that corner that I don't think about those evenings in the past when I've caught catfish. In a sense, this corner has an invisible monument to catfish. How about you? Do you have any of these unseen markers along a favorite stream, or located on a lake where you once caught a nice one?

Now monuments to fish are fine, but it's far more important that each of us has a specific spiritual marker. Is there a place where you can clearly remember making a serious commitment to Jesus Christ? In the New Testament an Ethiopian eunuch came to know Christ while in a chariot (Acts 8), and for the Apostle Paul it was on a road to Damascus (Acts 9). For a lady named Lydia the Lord opened her heart next to a river (Acts 16).

I know of some who came to know Christ in a church pew while others gave their lives to God during a Vacation Bible School. Some have accepted Christ on or alongside busy highways after hearing the Good news of Jesus Christ shared on the radio. Many have become Christians in front of kitchen sinks, and still others at kitchen tables.

For me that crucial time of surrender to Christ began in a trailer house after watching a Billy Graham Crusade on television. God listened to my cry for forgiveness despite the marijuana plants growing on the kitchen table and pornographic posters tacked to the living room wall. Indeed, God's promise that, "Everyone who calls on the name of the Lord will be saved," (Romans 10:13) proved true. Despite my disgusting and perverse lifestyle the Lord listened to my desperate plea for His help.

But how about you? Do you have a spiritual marker? If not, establish one today—because, "now is the time of God's favor, now is the day of salvation" (2 Corinthians 6:2). After all, if the Lord of the universe was willing to listen to me—I know He will listen to you!

Prayer: *Heavenly Father, thank You for providing a way to have a second chance. May You be glorified in me and through me. I ask this in Jesus' name. Amen.*

MY CLAIM TO FAME
Scripture Reading: Psalm 139:1-12

Most hunters will miss a deer every now and then and I am certainly no exception. The truth of the matter is I've probably missed more deer than most.

Of course, hunters miss deer for a variety of reasons. Sometimes it's a small tree that jumps in front of the bullet, a twig that deflects an arrow, or a deer's reflex action which makes it appear they have successfully ducked the arrow. Nevertheless, often the only valid explanation is that the hunter simply missed. Many have seen video or television footage of a whitetail narrowly escaping a hunter's bullet or arrow. However, I've managed to accomplish something that few hunters in the world ever will.

My "claim to fame" began with a phone call from Jeff Horwich, a reporter for Minnesota Public Radio (MPR). While on the Internet he had come across the Christian Deer Hunters Association® website. Since I am the founder and executive president of the association, Jeff wanted to go along on a hunt with me as part of an interview for a story.

At first I was a little apprehensive. Although I frequently listen to MPR and find many programs informative, Jeff was not a hunter, and he had never been on a hunt before. Would he be fair, or would he misrepresent both the hunt and the ministry of the Christian Deer Hunters Association®? Even so, we set a date for him to accompany me on an archery hunt a couple of days after the Minnesota deer gun season ended. I also asked Kent Rydberg, the membership coordinator for the association to come along.

Although I hunt almost exclusively on public hunting land I wanted to find a piece of private property for an evening hunt. Hunting on private land would allow me to set up a couple of portable tree stands the day before (something currently not lawful on public land). Our church pianist, Cheryl Jakobitz, asked a neighbor if I could hunt on his property for one day—and he agreed.

It was a cold and windy November afternoon when we arrived at the patch of woods. Kent would go in on one side of a creek and set up his stand, while Jeff and I would crawl up into the two portable tree stands I had hung the day before. Jeff sat with his mike and recorder, I with an old recurve bow. My claim to fame soon followed. Here is some of Jeff's play by play report:

> For an hour we sit in dead silence twenty feet apart, and fifteen feet off the ground. Then, behind us some rustling. Rakow tenses. His bow string drawn back to his shoulder. [There is the faint sound of the shot]──Rakow's trailing string winds off into the brush.

I missed! I choked! I blew the shot! I ended up trimming some hair off the deer's back, but thankfully did not wound him.

Now I want to ask you, "How many people do you know who have missed a deer on the radio?" Yes, my claim to fame (or rather infamy) is that I am one of only a few people in the world (if not the only one) to have ever missed a deer on the radio!

When the program aired, I discovered there had been no need to worry about Jeff Horwich's reporting. He did an excellent job of conveying the ministry of the Christian Deer Hunters Association®, as well as accurately depicting the hunt itself. Jeff objectively reported the facts—and my missing the deer happened to be one of those facts. As a result, the account of my hunting blunder was not only heard in Minnesota, but now a number of years later it can still be listened to on the world wide web. Yes, sometimes the things we fail at can end up getting a lot of exposure.

But did you know that according to the Bible there is coming a time when every single thing we have ever said or done are going to be exposed? Now it is one thing to miss a deer on the radio, but it is quite another to contemplate having one's secret words and moral failures broadcast before the world. Jesus warned, "But I tell you that men will have to give account on the day of judgment for every careless word they have spoken" (Matthew 12:36). Later, the Apostle Paul charged the Christians in Corinth to be careful to minister with right motives. He stated that when the Lord Jesus returns, "He will bring to light what is hidden in darkness and will expose the motives of men's hearts. At that time, each will receive his praise from God" (1 Corinthians 4:5b). Yes, God even weighs our motives!

How about you? Are there things in your life you would hate to have exposed? It is wonderful to know that we can bring our failures to God—and He will forgive us and cleanse us. God's word promises, "If we confess our sins, he is faithful and just and will forgive us our sins and purify us from all unrighteousness" (1 John 1:9). Not only that, but God also chooses not to remember our shortcomings. As the writer of the book of Hebrews states, "For I will forgive their wickedness and will remember their sins no more" (8:12). When we allow God to erase our sins, we don't have to live in dread of having them displayed in the future.

Prayer: *Heavenly Father, help me to live each moment in the light of Your presence. I ask this in Jesus' name. Amen.*

ELK HUNT
Scripture Reading: Numbers 9:15-23

It was my first archery elk hunt and my friend Kent and I were both excited. We drove my old, rusty van from Minnesota to Colorado and laid down a hefty price for a non-resident license.

A week earlier, a friend who lived in the area assured us that the elk were active on the mountain we would be hunting. Setting up camp at about 10,000 feet—we hunted down during the day and made our way back up the mountain at night. Nevertheless, after a couple of days of hunting it became abundantly clear the elk had moved out of the area. So, we began looking in other locations.

To be where the elk were we knew it was necessary to relocate. Although it didn't happen until we were on our way home—we did wind up spotting a few elk and plenty of fresh sign.

In the end, we both came back home without ever releasing an arrow at an elk. Nevertheless, there was something truly wonderful and refreshing knowing we were close to elk.

The Bible tells us that during the days of Moses the Israelites were able to follow a pillar of cloud by day and a pillar of fire by night. In order for the Israelites to be with God, they found it necessary to be where God wanted them.

When the Hebrews came out of Egypt, God guided them with a cloud. We are told, "Whether the cloud stayed over the tabernacle for two days or a month or a year, the Israelites would remain in camp and not set out; but when it lifted, they would set out" (Numbers 9:22). To be where God was manifesting His presence, they needed to move when and where God wanted them to move.

In the Bible, a believer's life is often described as a

walk. For example, John told his readers, "If we claim to have fellowship with him yet walk in the darkness, we lie and do not live by the truth. But if we walk in the light, as he is in the light, we have fellowship with one another, and the blood of Jesus, his Son, purifies us from all sin" (1 John 1:6-7).

The Christian life is also described as a race. Running in God's race requires us to "run with perseverance the race marked out for us" (Hebrews 12:1b). Friend, are you walking the walk and running the race?

You see, it's not God's desire that we live in the past where God has been at work. He wants us to walk close to Him right now. Some people turn to the traditions of the past. They think that if they attend a church where they grew up, or practice some long-standing ritual they will be all right. But the Bible never states this.

Friend, we are called to be doing what God wants us to do right now. We can't hide in the traditions of the past and then expect to experience God's presence in a powerful way. The God of the universe is a living God—not some lazy or lethargic deity. He is dynamic and powerful, not stagnant and stale.

Are you where God wants you to be? Are you (at this exact moment) doing what God is calling you to do? If not, step out in faith and follow Him.

Prayer: *Lord, help me to be dynamic like You! May others look at my life and be able to know that I am walking the walk and running the race for Your glory. In Jesus' name. Amen.*

Devotions for Hunters & Anglers

OFF THE BEATEN PATH
Scripture Reading: 1 John 2:7-11

It was five minutes before the close of shooting hours when suddenly, out of the corner of my eye, I caught a glimpse of a black bear silently making its way through thick undergrowth. The bear stopped about thirty-five yards away. I pulled up the 30-06, "Boom!" The bear dropped. Later I would find out that this solitary sow was sixteen-and-a-half years old (in Minnesota successful bear hunters are required to send in a tooth sample by which the bear is then aged).

However, by the time I took down my portable tree stand, tagged, and then field dressed the bear it was dark. Furthermore, I then discovered my flashlight was so dim it was practically useless. Not wanting to misplace my rifle or tree stand in the dark—I decided to haul the tree stand, rifle, and bear all out in a single trip up the steep hill. I had taken bear off this particular stand before, so I figured I could "feel" my way along the trail and out of the woods. Besides, all I had to do was keep going up hill and I would eventually come to a gravel road near where my old van was parked.

Nevertheless, somehow I missed a small turn and got off the trail. However, when a car drove by on the gravel road further up the hill I knew I was veering to the right. The car's head lights made it clear I needed to make a major correction to get anywhere near the trail. But when I did, I ended up not going far enough to the left. Believe me, it's not easy dragging a bear uphill through thick brush with a tree stand hung on one shoulder and a rifle sticking up over the other.

When I finally got to the top of the hill, I was totally exhausted. However, a couple hunting in the same state forest with me, Reverend Gerald and Thelma Hintz, drove back on the dead-end road to make sure everything was all right. Thankfully they helped me load the bear into the back of the van.

    I have since retraced the route I took out of the woods that night and I don't think there could have been a worse path to take. I had drug the bear uphill through the middle of a big treetop, thick brush, and over a large boulder. Even so, all of this could have been avoided if I would have had a decent light to reveal the path.

    Just as a flashlight or lantern can keep us on the right trail, so also God's word can give us clear direction and divine discernment. The psalmist told the Lord, "Your word is a lamp to my feet and a light for my path" (Psalm 119:105). God's word keeps us from all kinds of traps and pitfalls. Still, not everyone wants to use God's light. Not everyone wants to walk in the path that He has wisely marked out for us. As a result, we can encounter certain difficulties we don't really need to experience. The book of Proverbs states, "The way of the unfaithful is hard" (13:15b).

    How about you? Are you using the light God has made available? Are you regularly reading the Bible? If not, start studying the Scriptures today. After all, Jesus not only knows the way, He is "the way" (John 14:6).

Prayer: *Heavenly Father, help me to stay on the path You have selected. I ask this in the name of Your Son—Jesus. Amen.*

ONCE IN A LIFETIME MOOSE HUNT (Part 1)
Scripture Reading: Proverbs 16:33

It was the culmination of a ten year dream. For nine long years I had faithfully applied for the Minnesota moose lottery. This is a drawing for a once-in-a-lifetime chance for residents to take any moose (bull, cow, or calf) by rifle or bow. Because I was not getting any younger, and the rheumatoid arthritis with which I was diagnosed was not getting any better—on the tenth year I decided to apply for a different zone. I hoped this would increase my chances of being drawn.

This new zone I applied for was entirely in the Boundary Waters Canoe Area. It had been recently formed when the Department of Natural Resources took the remotest areas of three other zones to make another new one. This meant no motors, wheels, or helpful devices for getting into the area, or for packing out a moose. Travel would be by canoe and on foot. Unlike the area for which I had previously been putting in—I knew nothing about this zone.

I was pleasantly surprised and extremely excited when notification that I had finally been drawn arrived in the mail. The church I pastor, Grace Bible Church, rejoiced with me and started praying for success. When my friend Jim Suttinger from Ohio found out that I had been drawn for a moose he made and sent me a dozen of the most beautiful wooden arrows I have ever seen. He weighted them especially for moose and then inscribed a Bible reference on each arrow. One of the references was Proverbs 12:27, "The lazy man does not roast his game, but the diligent man prizes his possessions."

Meanwhile I was shooting arrows, watching moose hunting videos, practicing calls, and learning all that I could in preparation for my once-in-a-lifetime hunt. Although I would haul a rifle along on the trip—my ultimate goal was to take a bull moose with a long bow.

    I did a couple of scouting trips to the zone and found a cow moose skull, and the fairly fresh remains of a moose calf which had evidently been killed by wolves. However, I found no fresh moose tracks or droppings on either of the scouting trips which caused me concern.

    The season arrived and I headed into the wilderness. A day later I was joined by my friends Art Sakaye, Tim Redingtom, and a new fellow by the name of Matt Witt. They all took time off work and at their own expense purchased provisions for the trip. Furthermore, they were committed to spending as much time as it took for me to take down a moose. According to Minnesota law they could not assist me in the actual hunt, but when I had harvested my big bull moose, Art, Tim, and Matt would help pack him out of the wilderness. They all had such a wonderful servant attitude even when the weather was less than pleasant. It either rained or snowed almost every day—and yet they kept a warm fire going, were constantly drying my clothes, loaned me their own dry clothing, and cooked excellent meals every night.

    We kept moving further back into the wilderness. Although we left some of the gear behind, we still had big loads to carry over difficult portages going from lake to lake. We had great talks and long theological discussions about the Bible, and each night they patiently put up with my preaching.

    They joked that they were going to convert me back to drinking. And although I was never tempted to drink, I must admit experiencing some of the greatest times of supernatural depression and spiritual warfare I have ever faced. This didn't happen in camp—only when I was out hunting. When I returned to the camp, the depression and suicidal thoughts would fade. In fact, in camp I felt empowered by God. This was strange because for me being alone in the woods is normally a wonderful and relaxing experience. I still can't explain this except to say that it was supernatural and that the powers of darkness were certainly present—even in the wilderness. It may be they merely wanted to stop the spiritual discussions we were having from taking place. Whatever the case, it continued on through the rest of that week. It was terrible. In fact, it kept getting more and more difficult to go out to hunt and then face the spiritual onslaught I was experiencing.

The hunting was also physically draining due to the wet and cold weather. There had also been a severe blow down in that part of the Boundary Waters a couple of years earlier. There were many times when I was either walking on fallen trees or crawling under and through them.

Each day my dream of harvesting a moose continued to dwindle. The first thing that went out the window was my high hopes of taking a big bull moose with the longbow. If need be, I would take my bull with a rifle.

Next my need to take even a small bull moose disappeared. After all, a cow was legal and would taste just as good, and maybe even better!

Even though I kept striving to succeed and my friends were more than willing to continue, after a week I knew it was time to take a break. Besides, the wet and cold weather was really getting to me physically. So, we broke camp and started on the journey home empty-handed. Inside I was striving and anxious. I could feel my once-in-a-lifetime opportunity to harvest a Minnesota moose slipping helplessly through my fingers. However, as we were paddling back out I inwardly knew I would have to try again just to make sure I had given it everything I had.

Prayer: *Lord, thank You for those who encourage and help us. May I be a source of comfort and encourage-*

ment to others. I ask this in Jesus' name. Amen.

ONCE IN A LIFETIME MOOSE HUNT (Part 2)
Scripture Reading: Ecclesiastes 3:1-8

A few days later I headed back into the wilderness alone. I paddled a one-person canoe and, along with my limited food and gear, had packed a rolled up inflatable raft which was large enough to transport a boned-out moose. Although a few years earlier I and a couple others had helped my friend Art Sakaye pack out his Pope and Young bull, I knew doing it all alone would pose a major problem. Whenever I started thinking about the difficulty of such a task, I reminded myself, "Packing a moose out is not a problem, but NOT having a moose to pack out IS a problem!"

I set up camp and invested the entire next day just looking for fresh moose sign. Starting out before daylight and making a fifteen mile plus hike over hills, through swamps, brush, and streams, I arrived back in camp just before dark. On the far end of my loop (about eight miles away) I had found a bull rub and at least two different sets of fresh tracks. At last there was some hope! Even so, on the inside I was still striving and concerned about blowing my once-in-a-lifetime opportunity. Time was running out.

To get near the fresh sign by canoe required a lot of paddling and about eight portages, so I opted to travel by foot. I moved camp closer, but it still took two-and-a-half hours just to walk from my new camp to the fresh moose sign. Nevertheless, I was desperate and this was the hottest place I had found to hunt.

Making the long trip back to camp the next evening I started contemplating how a smaller cow moose or a calf would be much easier to get out of this remote area. I started praying to that end. Better yet, maybe I could shoot a hollow moose! You know, something like those hollow milk chocolate bunnies stores sell at Easter time.

That night in my tent I was thinking about all the planning, preparing, and praying that had gone into this hunt. I thought of how my wife Beth, our girls, and the church had seriously prayed for me and spoken words of encouragement. Personally I had prayed for this opportunity to hunt moose for many years. I thought of Art, Tim, and Matt and how they'd spent time and money to help me out. I thought of numerous others who had loaned me equipment and even canoes so I could make the trip. Nevertheless, now it was looking more and more hopeless. My once-in-a-lifetime opportunity to hunt moose was rapidly going down the drain. Yes, time was running out. But then something happened that put things in their proper perspective.

That night as I lay in my tent alone, I was turning the dial on my transistor radio when I picked up a Christian radio station on the skip. I only heard about three minutes, but it was exactly what I needed. It was a call–in program with Joni Erickson Tada as the guest. Joni is a quadriplegic who (despite her physical disability) has ministered powerfully to multitudes. Joni had written a book, and a male caller (perhaps someone also with a disability) had phoned to tell her, "I really appreciate what you had to say in your book. Especially where you state that there are more important things in this life than being able to walk."

Friend, I want to tell you that those few words from that caller regarding Joni's book immediately changed my perspective. Although I was in a remote part of the wilderness where no wheelchair could travel, God chose to use a quadriplegic and an unknown caller to speak to me. I thought, "Surely if there are more important things in this life than being able to walk, there are also a whole lot more important things in life than Tom Rakow harvesting a moose!" From that point on, the pressure was off and I started truly enjoying the hunt. The lakes seemed clearer, and the colorful fall leaves much brighter.

But as a wise man once said, "There is a time for everything, and a season for every activity under heaven" (Ecclesiastes 3:1). Indeed, there is "a time to search and a time to give up" (Ecclesiastes 3:6a). On the fifth day of this second attempt I headed back home with no moose. However, I did possess a far greater appreciation for the unique opportunity I had been given to go on a "once-in-a-lifetime moose hunt."

Prayer: *Heavenly Father, thank You for speaking to us through other people. Amen.*

MEADOWLARK LAKE
Scripture Reading: James 4:13-17

  It was a beautiful June day along Meadowlark Lake in the Big Horn Mountains of Wyoming. We were on vacation. A death in the congregation I pastor had caused me to postpone our leaving Minnesota a couple days. But now, here we were in the Big Horn Mountains fishing along the bank and near the outlet of this picturesque high altitude lake—away from death. Our girls were busy catching rainbow and brook trout. We had been there about an hour when a friendly couple (who looked to be in their fifties) passed by and the man began fishing. After a while the lady walked past and headed back up to the picnic and parking area some one-hundred-and-fifty yards away. But then a little later this same woman came back past us making a friendly remark. After briefly visiting her husband further down the lakeside bank she again came past us and went back up the hill.
  Moments afterwards my wife Beth came running, "Tom! There is a woman on top of the hill dying!"
  We both rushed up to the parking area. There, lying on the gravel road between two vehicles was the lady who just minutes earlier had walked past. Her sister, an RN, was desperately giving her mouth-to-mouth while her brother-in-law was doing compressions on her chest. Her husband, wearing a fishing cap and vest, kept gently caressing his wife's hair and saying, "Come on, honey! Come on, sweetheart!" Beth kept checking, but could not get a pulse. Furthermore, due to the remoteness of the lake it took about forty minutes (which seemed like hours) for the ambulance to finally arrive. We later learned from an obituary posted on the Internet that the woman was fifty-seven years old.
  Friend, if I had known how soon this woman would be stepping into eternity—I would have done everything

possible to make absolutely certain she was ready. However, according to the Bible, no human knows what the immediate future holds. The book of Proverbs states, "Do not boast about tomorrow, for you do not know what a day may bring forth" (27:1). Again, in the New Testament James warned his readers,

> Now listen, you who say, "Today or tomorrow we will go to this or that city, spend a year there, carry on business and make money." Why, you do not even know what will happen tomorrow. What is your life? You are a mist that appears for a little while and then vanishes (4:13-14).

This event at Meadowlark Lake had an immediate, yet profound, impact upon me in a number of ways. First of all, there were ten or twelve anglers who were standing nearby observing this sad event. A couple of them were visibly shaken. I also knew without a doubt God was compelling me to seize this unique opportunity to share Christ with them, so I did. Indeed, I had a renewed sense of urgency to share the Good News of Jesus with any who would listen.

Through this tragedy I was also reminded of how quickly a loved one can be taken away. It was obvious that this heart-broken husband had not realized that this woman whom he openly loved would soon be gone. In the days that followed I hugged my kids a little harder and held my wife a little longer.

But how about you? If your life ended this very day, would you be ready to meet your Maker? Of course, none of us knows exactly when or how our lives on this planet will end. However, when we truly come to Christ we can be confident that we will never have to face condemnation. Jesus said, "I tell you the truth, whoever hears my word and believes him who sent me has eternal life and will not be condemned; he has crossed over from death to life" (John 5:24). Have you passed over? If not, call on Christ today!

Prayer: *Lord, help me to live each minute as though it is my last. In Christ's name. Amen.*

Helpful Outdoor Ministries

Christian Anglers Association
PO Box 142
Silver Lake, MN 55381
http://www.christiananglers.net

Christian Bowhunters of America
3460 West 13th St.
Cadillac, MI 49601
http://www.christianbowhunters.org
616-775-7744

Christian Deer Hunters Association
PO Box 432
Silver Lake, MN 55381
http://www.christiandeerhunters.org
1-866-HIS-HUNT

Farmers and Hunters Feeding the Hungry
216 N. Cleveland Ave.
Hagerstown, MD 21740
http://www.fhfh.org
301-739-3000

God's Great Outdoors
8193 Emerick Rd.
West Milton, OH 45383
http://www.ggoutdoors.org
1-877-TALK-GGO
Other important ministries can be found at this website.

Rock Dove Publications Order Form

___ *"Copy Me!" Bible Quizzes (Twenty Reproducible Quizzes!)*: $19.95

___ *Messianic Psalms: An Inductive Bible Study*: $5.95

___ *Devotions for Dog Lovers*: $7.95

___ *Hunting and the Bible: A Scripture Safari*: $3.95

___ *Self-Inflicted Hunting Arguments*: $12.95

___ *Devotions for Hunters & Anglers*: $14.95

___ *The Prodigal Pooch* Tract (pack of 100): $8.95

___ *Raccoon Hunting Questions* (audio tape): $9.95

Shipping free in the USA. Otherwise add $2. Minnesota residents add 6.5% tax.

1) Call toll-free 1-888-HIS-DOVE.
2) Order online at http://www.rockdove.com
3) Mail this form with name, address, and payment to:
   Rock Dove Publications
   PO Box 203
   Silver Lake, MN 55381

TOTAL ENCLOSED_____